Understanding The Church

UNDERSTANDING THE CHURCH

Upon This Rock I Will Build My Church

R Lindemann

Aleph Publications
Wisconsin, USA

Aleph Publications
Manitowoc WI

Paperback Edition
ISBN13: 978-1-956814-36-1

33 32 31 30 29 28 27 26 25 24   2 3 4 5 6

Disclaimer

All information, views, thoughts, and opinions expressed herein are those of the author(s) and are being presented only for your consideration and should not be interpreted as advice to take any action. Any action you take with regard to implementing or not implementing the information, views, thoughts, and opinions contained within this published work is your own responsibility. Under no circumstances are distributor(s) and/or publisher(s) and/or author(s) of this work liable for any of your actions.

Anyone, especially those who have been victim of misdirected explanation and understanding, may be best served seeking wise counsel before deciding to implement any information, views, thoughts, opinions, or anything else that is offered for your consideration in this work. All information, views, thoughts, and opinions in this work are not advice, directive, recommendation, counsel, or any other indication for anyone to take any action. All information, views, thoughts, and opinions offered herein are offered only as suggestions for your personal consideration, which is done of your own free will. Your life is your own responsibility; use it wisely.

Any use of trade names or mention of commercial sources is for informational purposes only and does not imply endorsement or affiliation.

Please note that most of the items in quotes in this book are from various versions of the Bible and some quotes may have been paraphrased.

Dedication

When writing a book about the Church there is truly no one more appropriate to dedicate the book to than Jesus The Christ who is the Groom of the Bride-Church. So Jesus, this Book is dedicated to you. It is my prayer and hope and my belief that the words in this book will touch the slumbering hearts of many to awaken them to your Glory so that we may become the pure Bride-Church that you have for so long been seeking.

Contents

xii

Acknowledgements

With considerable time spent discussing the topics surrounding this book, I would like to offer my gratitude to those who engaged in many such discussions with me. Deep discussions regarding religion tend to get quite esoteric while bordering on the political and religious and can run amuck quickly when we lose focus. So, a big thank you to everyone who has taken time to discuss these very important topics with me, and for keeping me on topic during those discussions.

Introduction

Many of the topics in this book have been in my head for decades being thought upon every now and again to try to best understand what religion is and, more to the point, what the "Church" is about. Where did it come from and what is its purpose, and for that matter, what does the word "church" even mean?

The Church has its dogma and all sorts of rules and regulations concerning the "sacraments", but do these rules matter to people outside of the church? Will you "go to hell" if you're not part of the Catholic church? There's a balance in life and in Truth regarding the church and its reach and limits within our lives.

Does the Church trespass against us? Does it lead us into temptation? Between the point at which I decided I needed to write this book, and the time I actually began to write it, things changed—a lot! But the truth is that things did not really change much during that time, rather things were *exposed* during that time and those changes did somewhat effect the content scope of this book.

While the exposures of the church have been devastating to the church and will be partly addressed, this book is not about those issues. This book is here to help others to better understand what the Church is and what the purpose of the Church is and whether or not we are a part of it. But if we are not a part of it, then when can we become a part of it? And exactly how do we do that? With Baptism? First Communion? Marriage? What makes someone actually be part of the Church? And further, do we even want to be a part of the Church?

The answer to all of these questions begins with a simple statement: It all depends. So, what are these questions dependent upon? To answer that we must try to understand what exactly the "Church" is.

Before reading on, ask yourself right now: What do you currently say that the Church is? In a single sentence, how would *you* explain the Church?

Chapter 1

Conceiving a Church

What is "The Church"? It's likely not what most of us think it is. To begin to Understand The Church and the whole point of it, we first have to acknowledge that there is a Creator who we refer to as "God". This means that we have to back up a bit all the way back to Creation. Was the universe Created or was it an accidental occurrence? If it was accidental or somehow just happened and there is no God, then there's less need for a book like this one. Yet, even to a great extent, Understanding the Church can be done outside of the whole Creator/God aspect. Although without God, regardless of what the "Church" is, it would not exist today in any form.

When discussing subjects like religion and politics, we all tend to get a bit defensive when even the smallest detail of our chosen belief is pointed out as an error. But is it justified that anyone would get defensive when the conversation is only working to find the truth? What if the other person has a specific point that makes us feel somewhat defeated, is it not best then to listen to them and hear them out? It occurs all too often where when one of our erred details is pointed out to us it tends to undermine our *entire* belief system, thus causing us to depart from *all* of our beliefs. If our faith cannot withstand a few of our erred details being weeded out of our thinking, then that is an indication that our belief system was based solely upon dangerous blind faith, proving that our entire belief system was dependent solely upon those few details–This is never a good thing.

You can go into almost any religion's service, even if it is not a Christian religion, and you're going to hear things that are true and good, so we must not toss everything out just because we're wrong about a couple of details in our beliefs. Everyone needs to understand that if our entire belief system can be crushed by removing a couple of petty points, then we were not following God. In that case we were instead following mankind's rules and mankind's beliefs. Everyone has a right to their own opinion and interpretations, but always remember that no matter how sincere or authoritative someone else's beliefs sound to you, it is you and you alone that choose to believe them or not to believe them. So the views thoughts and opinions of others should be heard and considered, but not necessarily followed.

We need to be discerning when we discuss and consider these weighty topics. Even in this book, some points might sound harsh to you if any of those points happen to touch on something you idolize about your religious faith or beliefs. When a house is infested with rodents we don't burn down the entire house, we simply remove the unclean problem so that we can once again live in a clean home.

One Discerning Creator

Let's start from the very beginning. To try to get a grasp on the Creator/God, we need to consider what a "God" is. God is basically Good. God is a higher being who is the way to all good things. This term "God" is our human way of understanding a *Being* that is beyond us and is higher or more perfect than us. We could say that God is superior to us, but this allows for us to improperly believe that we are "gods" if we happen to be intellectually superior to someone else. Those who made themselves out to be gods in past millennia have all gone the same way—they all died typical human deaths. While someone can consider themselves a "god" because they might be more brilliant than most people are, they still fall short, very short, of the one True God. In other books that I have written I like to refer to this Creator/God as "The Creator" because that term eliminates potential confusion, but in this book we will mostly stick to the more familiar term, "God".

The idea of a "Creator" is truly key to Understanding the Church. The Creator God is said and believed to have Created everything even up to the point of making humans. Once we humans came onto the scene, then we too could create life, though not in anywhere near as spectacular a manner as God did, and not without God's prebuilt framework. The books *Bending the Ruler* and the various *The Science of God* volumes dive deep into those Creation topics. The level of intellect and discernment required to invent and then Create the fundamentals of matter is inconceivable to us humans. While we might pretend to understand it all, we actually don't, though we might try.

The point being made here is that the Creator, or God as we affectionately call the Creator, is really quite grand beyond our human ways. And this God is the basis of **ALL**, that is to say everything and everyone that is now or ever has been. In the first couple sentences on the very first page of the Bible, "God Said" and then it was. This discerning Creator spoke and then things came to be. But as discussed in the previously mentioned books, it was likely not a "let there be" statement and then POOF! suddenly everything was there as is often asserted by preachers, as well as by some science people's interpretation of the text even if they don't believe it themselves.

No, this God is a discerning and thinking God who contemplates and decides and then acts, much the way we humans do in the likeness of God. The Catholic Catechism indicates "That by faith we understand that the world was created by the Word of God, so that what is seen is made out of things that do not appear." But using pure logic we can easily conclude that we do not need such blind faith to understand that the world was created by the Word of God. This is pretty obvious if you allow yourself the depth of contemplation to imagine going from nothingness to a tangible world that we can touch and feel.

Planted Seeds

One of the first questions about the Church is, when was it actually established? Was it around 300 or 400 AD? Or was it maybe around the time of the Council of Trent? Or was it much, much earlier?

A lot of this has to do with what we want to consider "The Church". Since The Christ is said to be The Living Word of God and that Word of God is the same Word that spoke all things in to existence, we can then assume that the Church may a bit older than we typically think of it. Maybe not the Church in its current form, but the seeds where certainly planted during the Creation events.

Nurturing the Seeds

The first person in the Church congregation was, of course, Adam, and shortly thereafter Adam was joined by Eve. If you haven't heard the story, after creation was complete, God planted a Garden, and God placed two trees in the midst of the Garden of Eden. One Tree was the Tree of Life and the other Tree was the Tree of the Knowledge of Good and Evil. Then God placed Adam and Eve in the Garden of Eden and instructed them that they could eat from any tree, but the Tree of Knowledge of Good and Evil they were not to touch or eat from because if they did they would surely die. No big deal, live in Paradise for free and live forever! Just don't eat from that one little tree over there or you'll die. But alas, as our human nature would have it, our curiosity got the best of us.

The "Serpent" entered into Garden and sought Eve, asking her why she was told to not eat from that particular tree. Eve had no problem not eating from that tree, she didn't even question it until she was asked, to which she responded that if they were to eat from the tree they would surly die. But then the Serpent beguiled her and said "You will not surely die. God doesn't want you to eat from the tree because then you will become like God knowing between Good and Evil.", which in fact was partly true. So, Eve's curiosity, one of humanity's greatest gifts and also one of our worst enemies, got the best of Eve and she did eat the fruit thereof and her eyes were opened. Then she proceeded to offer the same fruit to Adam, and he also did take and eat and his eyes were opened as well, with both now knowing good from evil.

Shortly thereafter, God entered the Garden seeking Adam and said, "Adam, where are you?" Imagine this as similar to when we play hide and seek with young children and say in that sing-songy manner "Where are you?" while deliberately not finding them because we know exactly where they are. Then Adam replies, "I was hiding because I was afraid because I was naked." Then God asks Adam, "Who told you that you were naked?" Adam responds, "The women you put with me gave me of the fruit of the tree." Then God asks, "Woman, what have you done?", to which Eve replies, "The Serpent deceived me." Then God addressed the Serpent and said "For this you shall crawl on your belly and strike at the woman's heel and she will crush your head." Upon this Adam and Eve were cast out of the Paradise, but God left them with a unique and very special message.

Conveying a Message In Us

Mankind is God's pinnacle of Creation, that is to say the final and perfect Creation in God's own image they were created. God was not going to let them go to waste and die off to never be again. No, all of God's creatures are special with the notable prominence of mankind. God made a promise to Adam and Eve when God put them out of the garden; God said "I will send my Word through your righteous offspring to save you." Through this righteous person God would come to redeem all the willing of man, and as a sign through the seed of Adam many years later God's Word made flesh would take on many other similar torments that Adam suffered at the hand of Satan. This message is buried deep within every offspring of Adam and Eve. Adam and Eve's offspring have for many generations awaited this righteous person who would redeem them from death. So, why does any of this matter to us?

There either is a Self-Created Creator or there is not a Creator. When one pulls one's head out of the sand, it is blatantly obvious that there is a Creator, and it is that God who is referenced in the Bible. It is the primary purpose of the Bible that we can learn about this Creator and Salvation. All of mankind did not descend from apes or monkeys, rather man descended from Adam and Eve, the first two Created of man. The seeds had been planted, and so The Church began long before the arrival of The Christ, but was not yet established in any formal manner.

Chapter 2

A Church is Born

When observing mankind you will find that we often miss God's messages whether it's through our deliberate ignorance or through our utter blindness. The dialog that God had with Adam, which is found in extra-Biblical texts, is truly an important text. There's a far more detailed account of the life of Adam and Eve describing the time after they were cast out of Paradise than is shown in the Bible alone.

The Bible is a very brief history of the seeds God planted in us, and these extra-Biblical books shed additional light on the seeds of The Church and what was to come. As a matter of fact, without these additional textual accounts, the Bible would never have acquired the prominence it now has. It is unlikely that any of the books within the Bible would ever have been penned without that prior knowledge being carried forward. This extra knowledge was so common in the early days of humanity that there was no need to include it with anything.

You can think of the Bible as the short-notes that someone might use to pass the final exam in school. Yes, there are a great

deal more books about the particular line of history that the
Bible shows. The problem that many of us have when reading
these extra-Biblical books is that we are unable to discern which
are valid and which are not, or which have been irreparably
altered so as to make the Bible appear wrong. To press an
important point here, the Bible is the standard. It is the answers
to the final exam. Sure, there are some inconsistencies found in
modern Bible translations, which are discussed in *Understanding
The Bible*; but those inconsistencies are largely translation errors
and/or our own interpretation errors of the already translated
text. And of our own interpretation errors there are many!

In the Adam and Eve account, the Word of God told Adam
what would happen when the Word would come for them. You
could call it a prophecy, but since it is the actual Word of God
being conveyed to Adam it is of a unique nature and we will call
it a Promise or a Covenant. When Adam and Eve ate from the
fruit of the Tree of the Knowledge of Good and Evil, they did so
at the behest of Satan the Serpent. This means that they, of their
own free will, chose to follow Satan *instead* of God, which is why
God was so upset with them. Sadly, we fail to learn from their
mistake and often do the very same thing regarding our blind-
faithed religious beliefs—we follow lies, rather than God.

Existence

But why was Satan trying to deceive Adam and Eve to begin
with? Was Satan an innocent Serpent who was simply
questioning Eve about the Tree? Not likely. When Adam was
Created it was done after Satan the Moring Star was Created. Yes,
Satan was an Angel of Light named "Lucifer"—One of God's grand
achievements. But when God Created Adam, Satan was supposed
to bow before Adam because Adam was Created in the Image of
God. But Satan, being filled with jealousy and arrogance, would
not pay any homage to Adam, and for this Satan was cast down
to the lower world. Since Satan was still a prominent angel and
was given power over the lower realm of the world, when Adam

and Eve transgressed and followed Satan, *they chose* to follow Satan and place themselves under Satan's power. You could imagine this as being a parent and giving your children all good things, but then sending them off to school and you find that when they came home from school they have been deceived and have chosen to follow advice that is in dangerous contrast to your own good and loving parental advice to them.

Satan's goal was then, and still is today, to place humanity under his power. Satan wants to control us and to have power over us. You can easily spot someone who serves Satan rather than God by watching to see if they want to have *unjust* control over you. Satan wants power and control over us much the way many government officials and world leaders did through the centuries—and many still do even to this day.

At First Sin

While Adam and Eve lived briefly, but joyfully, in the Garden, a higher way to conceive spirit and life was readily within their grasp, but the moment Eve and then Adam even touched the fruit of the Tree of the Knowledge of Good and Evil they had sinned a grave error. The moment of first sin can be considered a genetic defect in all of their offspring—this includes us in this modern era. For us today it seems like no big deal because we have never experienced the higher state of mankind that Adam and Eve were originally created with. It's like written about in the book *Hot Water* where you have been in the water so long that you don't really realize how hot or cold the water is until the water temperature suddenly changes; when that change occurs, we become acutely aware of the change. For Adam and Eve they would have been basking in a pleasantly warm bath, and then the moment they touched that fruit and bit into it, the water instantly became hot—very hot!

It was at that very moment, in that split second, that they each submitted their life to Satan and were under contract with

Satan, thus losing the comfort and protection of a loving Creator God—it was Eternal doom! They subjected themselves to the one single entity, Satan, who hated them from the very start, and all with no escape and no end in sight. Who cares anyway, right? Well you do because, like it or not, you are offspring of Adam and Eve, and because of that you carry the gene of "Original Sin" with no escape.

The Committed Promise

Well that all sounds pretty depressing, but is it? It would be, but for one important point. That important point is the simple True and lasting Covenant that Creator God made to Father Adam and Mother Eve. God told Adam and Eve that God will send his Word through Adam and Eve's righteous offspring to save them at a later time. When God sends the Word forth, you can be certain it will occur as Promised.

Now, all that sounds fine, but how will we know when the Word finally arrives through one of Adam and Eve's righteous offspring? And how will we know who that offspring is?

Here is the point where additional reading can be of great assistance and also where prophecies come into the picture. God told Adam that as a sign for him when The Word made flesh comes through Adam's righteous seed, that the person who was The Word made into Man would take on him all of the perils that Adam experienced at the hand of Satan. Some people might take this to extremes and assume that Adam was crucified and died, but while incorrect, it is not really all that far off the mark, Adam did indeed die from a Tree of wood. Satan also tormented Adam and Eve and continually tried to deceive and kill them, but he didn't stop there. Adam's first son murdered Adam's second son at the prodding of Satan through Satan's effort to reduce and ultimately eliminate the newly forming population of man.

These things and many others, as well as the prophecies of the Bible, all point to the Promise of Salvation. When Adam asked how they could know who and when the Savior would come, he was told that as a sign the Word would take all that Adam had experienced at the hand of Satan on to himself. And that was the indicator of God's Committed Promise.

We Believe

"Belief" is an interesting topic. What exactly is "Belief"? To understand belief you must understand Love and to be loved. If you have a hard time wrapping your head around the concept of what real True Love is, then you will struggle to believe anything in a way that is full and robust as a child believes something. Sad to say, our humanity often does not lend well to love, and many people have been misdirected in this regard. Because of the lies of Satan, many homes are in disarray and wax cold. These homes lack love, and instead set up *things* of the world as their primary focus. This results in children who in turn don't get to experience true and full love from birth on, and all too often they never receive any real love from family, and therefore they rarely learn to offer True Love. This is why it is so easy for deviants to lure youth who have never been able to fulfill their inherent desire to be loved. When deviants open their arms to wounded souls, it feels so good to those wounded and empty souls because we all like to be accepted and feel wanted. Sadly, when this occurs, it's always to the destruction of the wounded soul, unless someone sees this occurring and cares enough to offer genuine love to that wounded soul. Our ability to *wholly believe* rests completely upon that simple truth.

When we are loved by another human, and I mean Truly Loved, we then can quickly find our way to believe. But to truly believe goes even beyond all of that. When you truly believe using full-faith, rather than using blind-faith, you then understand and thus you know certain things to be true because they are obvious and provable for you. People might debate the issue of somethings being "provable", but that is going to depend upon what evidence you will allow in your determination of things. When you learn how to Truly Love, it clears the heavy fog surrounding most of us. When that fog of lies clears and the Truth begins to shine forth, you will quickly come to see Truth.

The fundamentals of this Truth have even been put into a prayer or "creed". You can think of this as the super, super short version of the short-notes for the final exam. And for your convenience, here it is:

"I believe in God, the Father Almighty, Creator of Heaven and earth; and in Jesus Christ, His only Son Our Lord, Who was conceived by the Holy Spirit, born of the Virgin Mary, suffered under Pontius Pilate, was crucified, died, and was buried. He descended into Hell; the third day He rose again from the dead; He ascended into Heaven, and sits at the right hand of God, the Father almighty; from thence He shall come to judge the living and the dead. I believe in the Holy Spirit, the holy Catholic Church, the communion of saints, the forgiveness of sins, the resurrection of the body and life everlasting. Amen"

This is the fundamental creed of the church and it is the result of the seeds of which were just spoken of in this chapter, and it summarizes the fundamental beliefs of the Church, however it is missing some critical information that many people will want to know.

Chapter 3

My People Perish

It's probably good that we can boil down the core of God's Promises to a short prayer that can be read aloud in only thirty seconds. But then again, it's also a dangerous trap to get ourselves caught in. While it cuts right to the point, that prayer has little meaning to people without the rest of the Bible which explains the details regarding the story that the creed prayer is based upon. Even the Bible is lacking without the extra-Biblical books that exist, books which can be read by the willing.

In the Bible it says that "My People perish for lack of knowledge." Now don't confuse "lack of knowledge", with the Knowledge of Good and Evil. Knowing something is one thing, but knowing the difference between good and evil is on an entirely different level. Knowledge is one of those things that mankind seeks above all else, and the most prized bit of knowledge is to know God.

An Image of God?

We love knowledge, but we often trap ourselves in that knowledge. As society ebbs and flows, it goes wayward and then comes back to decency every couple of hundred years or so, which is easily discovered when studying history. The fact that we humans have been created in the Image of God is kind of a big deal—It is what sets us apart from God's other creatures.

This God-like nature is why we love knowledge—we want to know and learn. Just consider the amount of contemplation that God must have done to Create. It had to be a passion for The Creator to make such vast awesome beauty. Now in our human nature, just as we packaged the entirety of the Bible and Salvation into a Thirty-second soundbite, we also take the sum of human knowledge and pretend to teach all of it to unsuspecting youths as they enter the education system, especially regarding college. This is not necessarily a bad thing, but neither is it a good thing in and of itself.

The problem this causes is that far too many people who complete college have an erred understanding of "knowledge" as they make a blind assumption that upon graduating they now know everything. These "educated" people then go on to make rules and laws, and we all know how very badly that sometimes can end.

Some people say that the church is the image of God, and while that might be true, it was not true of the church in its state of condition early in the twenty-first century. We are human and in our humanness we try to know things. When we do this we try to set the standards by codifying our knowledge into a standardized set. The set might be a thirty second prayer, or a law of the land, or even the contents of a textbook. Those who establish and enforce those standards sometimes get a bit full of themselves.

The Drug of the Church

Did you ever attempt to read the entire sheet of warnings and instructions for any modern pharmaceutical drug? I didn't think so. These vast sheets of information are confusing and lengthy, and are sometimes made that way deliberately to obscure the horrific underlying truths about the drug's potential side-effects and also as a disclaimer of responsibility for the negligence of the pharmaceutical companies. Then doctors who dispense or prescribe these complicated drugs become the authorities on them, though it is unlikely that they read the entirety of such instructions themselves. But we believe that the doctor is the authority when it comes to our health, so we listen and do as we are told. The laws of our land are similar, they are complex and confusing, and the authorities of those laws are, of course, the lawmakers.

The Church does similarly. We humans are of the race of man and we like to make rules. When we get a bit too arrogant, we begin to make rules and enforce them onto others, but often we ourselves won't even bother to follow the rules we took part in making. These sorts of people love to consider themselves "authorities" on such matters and we tend to want them to do so, but are they authorities? "Authority" is derived from the word *author*. An author is one who writes. So in many cases the people who actually wrote the rule are the authority on that rule, yet those who follow in the footsteps of those true authorities often overstep their boundaries in enforcing those rules, as was witnessed in the early part of the twenty-first century.

According to the Bible, this authority problem is the part of humanity that The Christ disliked most. You would think with a church that is supposed to be following "The Good Shepherd" that the church leaders would seek the guidance of the words of The Christ Jesus and then proceed to **_not_** do the things that The Christ spoke against. But alas, this is not so. Some of the Leaders of the church are the worst offenders of this authority issue where they try to enforce and preach the rules, but are not even close to following those rules themselves. Authority is a drug to many church leaders, and they wield it like terrorists.

Magisterium and the Documents

Magisterium is the teaching authority of the Catholic church through the Pope and Bishops, and many documents have either been written or approved by them, documents that teach about certain beliefs of the church. While these documents don't change much over time, the reality is that if they change at all, it means that they were either inadequate to begin with or were somehow found to be flawed, or possibly subsequently even had errors inserted into them or Truth removed from them. This means that if people are being taught that which is contained in such documents, they then are possibly being taught incorrectly to some extent.

The problem with humans and church authorities is that we tend to forget about Truth, and instead we try to force upon others what *we* want to believe. Truth is not what you said, or I said, or she said, or he said, Truth is a mental and spiritual process that far too few people are taught. Knowledge without Truth will always end in lies and deceit. True Knowledge is based only upon Truth and it is highly sought after by most of man. However, due to our understanding of knowledge, or rather lack thereof, we tend to assume that when we have knowledge we then know the truth. But this is not so. In fact if you seek knowledge before Truth you are *not* likely to find Truth. Find Truth and then knowledge will be added unto you, which is encapsulated in Christ's words "Seek and you shall find". It is Truth that we are to seek, and true knowledge comes on its own when we seek Truth. Yet, while seeking, if we fail to explicitly seek Truth, we will most certainly find lies, of which there is no shortage of examples for us to study.

The Purpose of Joy

When we find Truth or even a glimmer of it, the Truth we found is to us a shining bit of gold worth incalculable value. It to us is True Joy. It is said that the Truth shall set you free. This is why we seek Love anywhere we can find it. Truth is a form of tremendous acceptance and when you find Truth it will draw you into a new way of understanding, thus allowing you to offer True Love.

Joy is often found in our spouse. We find a person who loves us fully and completely and they will offer themself to us fully and completely. It is full acceptance, full Truth between you two, and full Love—you believe in each other. If you ever wonder why marriages fail, you need look no further than to see what someone did to violate the basic rule said in this paragraph—and within those violations is also the fall of mankind.

Yet for many people this point of joy remains, and it is added to by giving birth and being able to give love to and receive love from the children of that true union. When a child is yet quite young we take them to be baptized, which is another point of joy. When we baptize our children we are acknowledging that they too can be accepted and redeemed as per God's Covenant with Adam and Eve. This is why baptism brings Joy to parents. But what does it mean? And what is the point of baptism?

Chapter 4

The Word Made Flesh

Why does anything in the first three chapters of this book matter when trying to understand the Church? It's because it all centers around Adam and Eve eating from the Tree of the Knowledge of Good and Evil and the subsequent Promise or Covenant made to Adam and Eve by God. God told Adam "I will send My Word through your Righteous offspring", and it was that Promise that began its fulfillment at what we call Christmas.

If you have not already noticed, take note that the word Christmas contains the word *Christ* and the word *mass*. While we might not have the celebration day perfectly laid out on the calendar, we do recognize this day as the celebration of the birth of The Christ who is The Word made flesh. That is to say, Christ is the fulfillment of the Promised Redeemer who saves Adam and Eve's offspring from the grasp of Satan and eternal death.

So what? It's just another baby man, right? Ah, but He's not *just another* man. This is where the story begins to get more interesting. Most people who read this will likely have heard about Baby Jesus whose Mother never had intercourse or sex—

she was a virgin and gave virgin birth to her Son Jesus The Christ. This means that Jesus did not have an earthly father. This is often depicted improperly in statues and illustrations, but Virgin Mary and Joseph never had sex and they were decades apart in age. Mary was a very young girl only about twelve or thirteen years of age and she was raised in the temple. When she was showing signs of becoming a woman, they wanted her protected because they knew that she was special. For this they gathered the good men of the Priests and they placed their staves on the alter to see which staff would spring forth buds, but no staff budded.

Then they sought to find out whose staff was missing, and found it to be Joseph the old widower who was advanced in years and who already had children of his own. He had no need to marry anyone, as that part of his life was completed to his satisfaction, plus Mary was far too young for him. Yet they insisted that he place his staff on the alter with the rest of them, and to his surprise it was his staff that then budded even bringing forth fruit. According to the prophecies this was a clear sign that it was he who was supposed to be betrothed to the young Virgin, and so they were betrothed. In case you're wondering, the word "betrothed" is rooted in *be-truth*, meaning to be true or be faithful. Not long after this Mary became pregnant, but it was not by the old widower Joseph her husband who she was betrothed to. Joseph was to be her protector, but while he understood this, I suspect he did not grasp the fullness of this until a bit later.

Mary was visited by the Holy Spirit. You can consider this Holy Spirit as The Word of God that would come through Adam and Eve's righteous offspring to save mankind. It is this Word who Created all things, and who came unto the young Virgin and made her with child. As Virgin Mary progressed in her pregnancy, Joseph was going to cast her away because he suspected that she had been with another man—but she had not!

When Joseph wouldn't believe Virgin Mary, he was visited in a dream or vision by an angel filling him in on the details.

Just to get a grasp on this, Joseph was likely old enough to be Virgin Mary's grandfather, and possibly even great grandfather. So for them, a sexual relationship was not in the picture. Parts of these events were spoken of many hundreds of years before they ever occurred.

Making a Way to Salvation

To begin to understand the "Church" you must understand Salvation. This little Baby was going to be The Redeemer of the world—for *all* of man. But what is He here to redeem us from? He had come to redeem us from the forfeiture of our freewill to Satan and our subsequent eternal death that were both inadvertently agreed upon by Eve and by Adam. This little innocent Child was somehow going to be our Salvation—that is to say, the Salvation of the entire world. It is uncertain how much they knew or were told by the angels about the little Baby Word made flesh, there are even ancient writings stating that Baby Jesus spoke while yet very young at the age of only one or two and maybe earlier. This was not referring to baby-talk but rather articulate statements that no typical child would have knowledge of.

This little innocent child would grow up to become the Man we now call Jesus The Christ. When yet a boy, Jesus taught in the temple and asked questions and answered questions, and as he grew older he began to show his true self by doing miracles. As he taught people and performed healings, ever more people began to follow him to hear his wisdom and the many simple Truths he spoke. But referring back to the "Drug of the Church" which is *authoritarianism*, the priests, scribes, and Pharisees (you can equate them to church leaders, news people, and politicians of the modern era), had a great amount of disdain for Jesus The Christ, and their jealousy caused them to seek his death.

These leaders in their own arrogance did not want Jesus to attract people who were under their control and draw the people away from the temple and to follow Him. They talked amongst themselves and in their misguided perception they decided that "it is better for one man to die than the whole congregation of the temple be lead astray." Not surprisingly, that is exactly what God wanted. God wanted for them to put this Word-made-Flesh to death to become the sacrifice God had promised to Adam and Eve. Although, as usual, God used their own arrogance against them, and Christ was indeed sacrificed. But this was not done to stop Him from luring the congregation away, rather, God allowed it in order to gather the True Congregation to him by being brutally tortured even worse than Satan had done to Adam, and He was tortured even as far as to die upon a wooden cross.

The Gate to Heaven

As a fairly young child I asked why Jesus died on a Cross, and was informed by the priest that "Jesus died for our sins." But the question was a bit deeper than that almost cliche part. The question was specifically meant as, why was it a *Cross*? A bit later in life I wondered why it was made of *wood*, and if any of that even matters? Why not some other material, what's the big deal about him dying anyway; people die gruesome deaths every day in this world? After lots of contemplation on the subject, I found that there is a reason that he didn't die in a car crash in the modern era, or was not killed in battle, etc. God has a way of doing things with a great deal of symbolic points, and it is those symbolic points that help us to confirm if that particular Man who died on the Cross was actually the Promised Redeemer. The greater the quantity of particular points introduced into any one prophesied situation, then the more difficult it becomes for any rational mind to refute its fulfillment.

The Cross was a *Cross*, not a tree as some would have you believe. Such lies are only distractions to cause us to doubt, thus resulting in our inconsistent understanding of the Bible. Such lies obfuscate the Truth within our minds so that we can no longer see the Truth that is born into all of us. Could the Cross have been made of, oh let's say, steel or metal, and still have meaning? No, it cannot.

To best understand this, you first have to take yourself back in time into the story to where there was only one rule in the Garden of Eden: Do not touch or Eat from the fruit of the Tree of the Knowledge of Good and Evil. We often get tripped up in the more important part of knowing between good and evil, causing us to miss the obvious fact that it was a Tree of *Wood*. It is Adam and Eve's violation of the rule regarding the Tree that caused their demise and damnation. And it was the *Wood* of the Cross that The Word Made Flesh was sacrificed upon to pay the penalty for that Original Sin of Adam and Eve.

But why a Cross? Well, that has two critical points to consider. The first is that the final letter of the ancient Hebrew script is in the shape of a lower-case letter t slightly tilted. Picture a Cross with one of its arms over your shoulder tilted, with the base dragging on the ground, much the way the Cross would have appeared as Jesus was carrying it over his shoulder. So big deal. right? It's just a cross that happens to look like the final letter of the ancient Hebrew Alephbet, there are lot of things shaped like that. Well, in Hebrew these ancient letters have a great deal of meaning. And the Final Letter of the Hebrew Alephbet is the *tau* or *tav*, or our modern English language letter, lower-case, "t" and it means the *end*, and *final*, and *perpetual*, and *promise*, and finally it means *Truth*. As a matter of fact, the Word *Truth* is tightly connected to all of that and is where the word and concept of Truth comes from, or we can more properly say that a *tav* or the Cross is the symbol of Truth.

Now, that all makes sense, the Cross is wood from a tree and so mankind was damned via a Tree and now is Saved via a Tree. And that Tree Wood was in the Shape of the letter tau or t which is at the end of the Hebrew Alephbet having the meaning of *Eternal* and *Promise* and *Truth*. This doesn't stretch any part to make things fit nor does it need to; it's just all simply the facts. You may assign whatever meaning to it that you wish, but those are the basic and true points of information regarding those things.

But yet there's still more to this story, not only was the Cross made of two parts, a post and a cross-beam, but it also has a connection to a door. Now this is not a big deal in itself because lots of things could resemble a doorway. But this is unique since that post and cross-beam are like a door post and lintel and on it hung the gateway or doorway by which you enter Heaven. Jesus said "No one can come to the Father except through me... I am the door". But it doesn't end there. After we begin to realize the many not so obvious but yet obvious things that God arranges, it would not be a bit surprising that it is possible that the Wood of the Cross was the exact same type of Wood as the Tree in the Garden, or for that matter Wood of the very same Tree, but of course that is only a speculative thought. You will find that God is quite entertaining in that way when you start to study the finer details of these types of things. It is in these details that we can know Truth.

Passing Over

If you have ever heard the story of the Israelites leaving Egypt, typically referred to as the "Exodus", you should recall that the angel of death came and killed all of the first born in Egypt. That night was the first "*Passover*". The Hebrews were instructed to take the blood of a perfect lamb and sprinkle it on the doorpost and lintel if they wanted their first born to live. And so they did, they took the blood of innocent perfect lambs and put it on the door posts and lintels of their dwellings. Then when the angel of death descended upon Egypt, the Hebrew Israelites were passed over by this angel, but the Egyptian homes which did not accept and bear the sign of the blood of the lamb on their door posts and lentil were not passed over, and the firstborn of each Egyptian family died that night.

So to connect this with the Cross and Jesus dying on the Cross, Jesus is considered to be the Lamb of God. In the Bible in reference to John the Baptist it says "The next day he saw Jesus coming toward him", and John said, "Behold, the Lamb of God, who takes away the sin of the world!" as Jesus approached. So the connection is that this "Lamb of God" was innocent and his Blood was shed upon the Cross as his blood flowed on to it and he died upon it. This then made Jesus the Sacrificial Lamb offered upon the Cross of Wood, thus the Eternal Promise to Adam and Eve was nearly completed. The Blood of the Cross is there so that death can *Passover* you. However, only when you accept the blood on the doorpost and lintel of the Cross will death pass over you, because if you reject and deny that Blood, then death still owns you.

When you accept the Blood of Sacrifice on The Cross into your heart and mind you are most of the way there, without that you will perish under the command of Satan. And as you might recall, Satan does not like *any* of man. It does not matter how good of a person you are, because if you reject the Blood on the Cross, then you have decided to **not** follow the simple and free instruction, and thus you have freely chosen to turn away from the doorway to Heaven in the same way that the Egyptians did. In that case you have freely chosen to reject the Covenant that God made with Adam and Eve. That particular Blood alone, and no other, is our key to the Kingdom. No matter how wonderful or how virtuous you are, you **cannot** enter Heaven without the simple and free acceptance of The Christ's Blood shed on the door post and lintel of the Cross so that you can make your way through the Door of Christ. And then as Christ said to the woman at the well, "Go and sin no more."

The Consignment to Peter

On the cover of this book you will see a picture of the "Consignment to Peter" where Jesus is handing a large key to Peter. Peter's birth name is Simon. He is often referred to as Simon-Peter. Jesus gave Simon the name Peter. Peter comes from the term *petra* like petrified, or rock. The name "Peter" has the same origin as the word "father" which is where term "padre" comes from. In ancient Hebrew, the letter "P" makes a "pfff" sound like it does in the German language beginning with lips together. Also the *tav* or "*t*" can make either a hard "*t*" sound or a softer "*th*" sound. So *pater* can be pronounced *pfather* or *father*. All of this points to *foundation* and a *firm base* on which to build. That is to say, a base that is strong and dependable. That's why men are called "fathers" and are to be the head of the household which is intended to be the rock and strength of the family, though sadly, that seems to have been fading in recent decades.

In our modern Bible translations Jesus said to Simon, "I will call you Peter for you are the Rock on which I will build my Church." But it would have been more on the order of, you are the pater (*or petra*) on which I will *establish* my Church, I will call you pater. The linguistic differences that we see in this are due to translation and phonetic changes. In our modern era language, Jesus was calling Simon a rock. The Christ Jesus trusted Simon the pater, that is to say Peter, enough to place him in a critical position at a critical time. This, of course, is as opposed to consigning this foundational task to someone who would run away the moment troubles came. It was to be given to someone who would have strong enough integrity to not lie, someone that The Christ trusted.

Simon-Peter did deny Christ during the events leading up to Christ's Crucifixion, so it could be said that he lied and ran away when troubles came. But that had to occur for prophecies to be fulfilled, and Simon-Peter's lapse in judgment helped Simon-Peter with his resolve in the years following. Upon Peter's hearing the cock crow, he immediately realized that he had denied Jesus The Christ just as Jesus had told him he would do. After all of the events unfolded and Jesus died, you can be certain that Peter was strengthened through his own failure. He learned from it, and now *we also* can all learn from *his* failure.

Chapter 5

Spirit of the Church

Peter was to be the solid foundation upon which The Christ would establish his Church, but what is this "Church" that was established upon Simon-Peter? What we today call "Christianity" flourished and floundered in its early days due to infighting and misinformation, some of which was deliberately inserted by those resisting the news of the arrival of The Christ. A few hundred years after the death of Christ the problems became so troubling that they had to come to an agreement on what would be taught and what they believed. So they formed a council at Nicaea and formalized a Creed of Nicaea or the basics of what they believed. This Creed has been slightly modified for articulation over the centuries, but has largely remained unchanged from its core principles. Here it is for your evaluation:

Breath of the Church

In its general form it reads as follows:

"I believe in one God,
the Father almighty,
maker of heaven and earth,
of all things visible and invisible.
I believe in one Lord Jesus Christ,
the Only Begotten Son of God,
born of the Father before all ages.
God from God, Light from Light,
true God from true God,
begotten, not made, consubstantial with the Father;
through him all things were made.
For us men and for our salvation he came down from heaven,
and by the Holy Spirit was incarnate of the Virgin Mary,
and became man.
For our sake he was crucified under Pontius Pilate,
he suffered death and was buried,
and rose again on the third day
in accordance with the Scriptures.
He ascended into heaven
and is seated at the right hand of the Father.
He will come again in glory
to judge the living and the dead
and his kingdom will have no end.
I believe in the Holy Spirit, the Lord, the giver of life,
who proceeds from the Father [and the Son],
who with the Father and the Son is adored and glorified,
who has spoken through the prophets.
I believe in one, holy, catholic and apostolic Church.
I confess one Baptism for the forgiveness of sins
and I look forward to the resurrection of the dead
and the life of the world to come.
Amen."

This creed is essentially the fullness of the Catholic church's core beliefs, and while the Catholic church claims its roots back to Simon-Peter as the father/pater/petra of the Catholic church, it is around the time of Nicaea that the more formalized church, as we understand it today, was constituted. That Creed is similar in function to The Constitution of The United States regarding what it means to its collective entity.

The Holy Spirit

But let us not get ahead of ourselves here. There are other events involved that led up to all of what was just discussed. "God", or this Creator, of which we have been speaking is not a human person like we of man are. God is obviously pure Self-Created Spirit and is quite intangible with regard to our scientific instruments. Spirit means *wind* or *breath* in its origin language, which is to say that spirit is not really able to be detected or seen, yet air flows all around you and it is everywhere. When The Spirit of God came to Christ's remaining Apostles as the Spirit came as "a sound from heaven as of a rushing mighty wind, and it filled all the house where they were sitting. And there appeared unto them cloven tongues like as of fire, and it sat upon each of them." Their new-found Truth gave them what was needed to really begin to build Christ's True Church.

The Our Father

As another core part of the Church, along with the creeds spoken of earlier, there was first "The Lord's Prayer" which Christ used as an example of *how* to pray:

Our Father, Who art in heaven,
Hallowed be Thy Name.
Thy Kingdom come.
Thy Will be done on earth as it is in Heaven.
Give us this day our daily bread.
And forgive us our trespasses,

as we forgive those who trespass against us.
And lead us not into temptation,
but deliver us from evil.
Amen.

This prayer is short and simple, and most Christian religions pray it at their daily and weekly masses. This particular prayer carries special significance to the followers of Christ because it was given to the Apostles by The Christ himself, and it has been handed down from generation to generation ever since.

Another prayer that tends to be more a specifically "Catholic thing" is the "Hail Mary" prayer. This prayer was assembled much later in around the 11th century; though the exact age is not specifically known. However, the greater part of it actually predates the Lord's Prayer or "The Our Father". When the angel appeared to the Young Virgin Mary to inform her that she would be the mother of the Redeemer, that Angel said to her "Hail, Mary full of grace, the Lord is with thee: blessed art thou among women". And when Mary went to visit Elizabeth her cousin, Elizabeth said to Mary "Blessed art thou among women, and blessed is the fruit of thy womb." Both women were pregnant at that time; Elizabeth was pregnant with John the Baptist who was Jesus' second cousin.

The prayer in its current form is as follows:

Hail Mary, full of grace,
The Lord is with thee
Blessed are thou amongst women,
and blessed is the fruit of thy womb, Jesus.
Holy Mary Mother of God,
pray for us sinners now
and at the hour of our death,
Amen.

A Point of Prayer

Prayer is an interesting topic, and while we call these short statement-sets creeds or prayers, we often miss the point of the prayer. The creeds and the Hail Mary prayer have been contrived by typical humans by taking statements and sentiments from the Bible and forming those words into the prayer form which they currently are. The Our Father prayer, that is to say the "Lord's Prayer", is different in that it was specifically given to the Apostles by the Christ who is The Living Word made Flesh, so the Lord's Prayer has very special meaning and significance. While this is not discussed in great detail in the book *Understanding Prayer*, the points made in *The Our Father* prayer are discussed. "Prayer" is not The Lord's Prayer specifically; rather this prayer is an example of how we can and should pray. Prayer is what occurs in the Lord's Prayer.

Let's briefly break it down:

Our Father, Who art in heaven: States that God is our father and resides in Heaven above (Regarding the concept of direction with Heaven being above, consider reading *The Science of God Volume 1* discussing that topic.)

Hallowed be Thy Name: A Proclamation that God's very Name is Holy.

Thy Kingdom come: Acknowledgement of The Kingdom of Heaven and its destination in us.

Thy Will be done on earth as it is in Heaven: Realization that what the Creator God intends to occur will occur both in the Earthly realm and in the Heavenly realm.

Give us this day our daily bread: Supply our needs for the day.

And forgive us our trespasses: Forgive us for the foolish errors we make.

As we forgive those who trespass against us: This one is trouble for us because many people are very unforgiving. And this confirms what Jesus said regarding judging people, "For with what judgment ye judge, ye shall be judged: and with what measure ye mete, it shall be measured to you again."

And lead us not into temptation: Keep us from evil and from harmful tempting things, people, and thoughts so that we do not fall to evil.

But deliver us from evil: And should evil come upon us, please save us from that evil because we alone cannot.

Amen: It is so, or so be it.

The 10 key points of The Lord's Prayer are as follows:
1. Recognize God the Creator.
2. Proclaim God's Holy Name to be Completeness and Holy.
3. Acknowledge Heaven.
4. Acknowledge God's Will.
5. Supply our needs of the Day.
6. Plead for forgiveness.
7. Recognize we will be forgiven only as we will forgive.
8. Ask for temptation to be kept away from us.
9. Plead for evil to be taken away from us.
10. And proclaim it all so.

While it is good to Recite The Lord's Prayer, or the "Our Father", we can make a pretty safe assumption that Jesus The Christ would rather have us understand the ten points being made, and then form a prayer of our own around those points, making it a personal prayer with deep personal meaning from each our own hearts that we offer unto our Father in Heaven. But for most people this is not the case because the prayer is said as if reciting a poem in a somewhat meaningless manner as a repetitive habit. It's not bad to do so, but if you want your prayers to really have power, then understand the ten points Jesus was trying to make in His prayer example. We should all reconsider our approach to prayer with these points in mind along with the understanding that is discussed in the book *Understanding Prayer*.

Chapter 6

Unity of the Church

Our ability to recite agreed upon creeds and prayers that are common to all of us is what brings and keeps us together as a people and as a Church. You can talk to a practicing Catholic, or any practicing Christian for that matter, anywhere in the world, and aside of the language barriers, they will also know the basic creeds and prayers. Think about that for a moment... this common thread throughout the entire globe binds together those who believe these creeds and prayers. In the United States and other countries we think that our Declarations and Constitutions are so wonderful, and most are, but they fail in comparison to the True creeds and prayers of the True Church. All of Christendom is unified through these beliefs. People should be in harmony, and it is these beliefs that tend to achieve that harmony when properly understood and abided by.

Atonement

"The World" has a stranglehold on most of humanity as it tries vehemently to draw us away from God. We must remember that

Satan was given dominion of this lower world in which we all live, and it is Satan's world that tries to draw us away from God. With all of the noise from the world, we lose sight of what things actually mean, which is especially true with *words*. From birth on we hear all sorts of terms, and as we grow we can generally use them properly without actually fully understanding those words. Take for instance the word "atonement", what does it mean? To "atone" is to make things right in our worldly eyes, and this is certainly true. But take a look at the word in this manner, *at-one-ment*. We are to be firmly *at one* with God, that is to say *at one* or *atone*.

When we properly understand the ten points of prayer mentioned in the previous chapter regarding The Lord's Prayer, or simple words like "atonement", it helps us to have a clearer view on what we are trying to achieve. We are to be ***at one*** with God. Think about that for a moment: it's a pretty grand notion that we can be connected with God so closely so as to be considered to be "*atone*" with God. This is similar to a husband and wife in the fullness of their marriage.

A Bride

A bride is to be a virgin all dressed in white and is intended to be clean and pure for her husband. But sadly in our modern era, many brides, and grooms for that matter, are anything but clean and pure, and the same is true of the church. The collective Church is to be the Bride of Christ, and we collectively are anything but pure and virgin for The Christ. You can think about it in this way: imagine yourself wearing pure white clothes. Now go to work and live your life in this world with those clothes for a day or two. Are those clothes still pure white, or might they be a bit dirty and maybe sometimes even absolutely filthy? Now consider your soul like that pure white dress or pure white clothes. Do any of us imagine that the pure white soul is pure white any longer after having lived in Satan's world that intends ill towards all man at all times? Not likely.

Not only does Christ's blood wash away the Original Sin acquired in the Garden of Eden, but accepting that Blood also washes away the filth of this world from our dirty souls to make them pure again and ready to be *at one* with Christ The Living Word.

Just as a bride gets all cleaned up and dresses in pure clean white so that she can be properly presented unfouled to her future husband, so too is this true of us. We need to make ourselves presentable or we will be rejected. What do you think would happen if a man was waiting at the altar of his wedding, and then after a bit of waiting his bride showed up stinking and dirty with her dress all shuffled and torn and dripping with filth. Do you think it would stop him at all? That probably would cause a bit of a pause before he would consider moving forward with the marriage, especially if she smelled of another man.

Marriage

When the bride is clean and prepared, she will be presented perfect to the groom to be married and the two become as one flesh. But what exactly is "marriage"? Is it the marriage certificate? Is it the legal binding statement some people make in front of a Justice of The Peace? Is it done through the authority of a priest in Church?

In our worldly view it can be all of the above. But marriage is far deeper than that. "Marriage", as we call it, is a binding of souls. The ceremony is referred to as a wedding, or to be wed. "Wed" means to *pledge* or to *promise*, and this "pledge" is made in front of family and friends. It is a pledge of *unity* or *oneness*. When a wedding occurs, we say that the bride and groom are married, but in truth they are not married at that moment, rather they both publically proclaimed to be wed at that time. Publically in front of family and friends they committed to this agreement. They *pledged* themselves to one another to be *at-one*.

The true marriage occurs during intercourse, when he "knows" her or enters into her in the most personal way. That is the True Marriage of the flesh of man and binding of souls. This means that the first person that you copulate or couple with, that is to say have intercourse with, is the person to whom you are or were married to in God's eyes. Beyond that, any subsequent people that you have intercourse with, whether you are married to them or not is, per the statements of Christ, considered adultery. This is why the idea of premarital sex has always been considered wrong and bad. If you are not willing to commit to each other in front of family and friends and God, then it is probably best to not engage in such intimate activities. And if you happen to be the type, whether man or woman, who promises "love" only for the purpose of "getting sex", then in a way you are a rapist. You need not look far to see the pathway littered with broken lives due to such abuse of marriage and violation thereof.

In our worldly human eyes, marriage is made lawful by a legal document that we sign, but with the Creator God, marriage is the binding of souls that occurs when a physical man enters into a physical woman. It is to be respected and used with love and care and devotion. When a man and woman have committed themselves to be "at one" with each other, they then can partake in such activities with each other as often as they both see fit. A truly lawful Godly Marriage is when a man and woman are truthfully committed to one another and copulate, or in engage in intercourse. This treasured intimate gift was given to mankind by God, and the abuse thereof is heralded by Satan's world as a good and virtuous thing, but such abuse of intimacy is neither good nor virtuous.

Christ said "You will know them by their fruits. Grapes are not gathered from thorn bushes..." Examine the tree of sexual immorality to see the kind of fruit that it bears and you will quickly realize its level of virtue, or rather lack thereof. Is the fruit from the tree of free sex good, or is it bad? We are to be clean and pure, and while we can wash ourselves in the Pure Blood of The Lamb of God and be cleansed from Original Sin, we must also remember that if we play in the dirty world we will get dirty. You can love a child and fully accept them because they love you, but good parents are not going to allow their children into the house to run freely unless they have washed the muddy dirt off themselves first. Do we imagine things would be any different with God?

There is a saying that goes "Cleanliness is next to Godliness." We must be clean. Cleanliness is stressed in the Bible and cleanliness goes a long way to keep disease and sickness away from any culture that follows good hygiene practices—The same applies to our souls.

If you observe the world, you will see that many areas of the world have thrived due to the cleanness of solid Christian principles. You also will notice that when those principles begin to diminish, so does the society as it drags its citizens along with it.

We must all keep ourselves as clean as possible and accept the Pure Blood of The Christ, and then we can be prepared to be *atoned* with Christ.

The Bride of Christ

What's the big deal, so what if we're not clean? We're here and alive and surviving, right? And what are we to be prepared for anyway, many of us are already married? The Church is the Bride of Christ. We are betrothed or be-truth-ed to The Christ. The Church is to be *at one* within itself and then the Church as a whole is to be pure and *at one* with The Christ. We are the Bride, that is to say we are the woman in regard to Christ. When we accept Christ in us we are at one with Christ individually, and when we are collectively at one with Christ, then the Church Bride is at one with Christ.

You might wonder how we can know if the Church is at one with Christ. Here we have a problem in that the Church's being the Bride of Christ is like becoming accustomed to a situation spoken of in the book *Hot Water* where we have been in that water so long that we barely realize that this is so. We are so accustomed to being the Bride of Christ that we fail to notice that fact. But in this late modern era, the water temperature is no longer at a comfortable level. We are beginning to notice that many churches are withdrawing from being a part of the Bride of Christ. And as the secular world of Satan slowly infiltrates the churches and introduces deception, debauchery, and outright lies, these churches are slowly, but at a rapidly increasing pace, divorcing themselves from The Christ.

If you think back to the beginning of this book and consider The Creator of everything and how one of that Creator's deepest desires is for us of man to be at one with The Creator, then being a clean Bride prepared for marriage makes a great deal of sense. It is what we all should strive for, and it is what we are made for. Just as Eve was made for Adam, we are made as companions and helpers for God.

Chapter 7

The Schism

When churches fall away it is a sort of "schism". They are divorcing themselves from The Christ. If you think about the seriousness of that, it is easy to see the error in it. "Divorce" means to *divert* or to *fall away*. Sometimes when a church falls away from Christ it is, in full technicality, divorced from The Christ. Divorce also happens within the church itself when people group together and the groups disagree with each other. When this occurs on a large or regional level where at one time they all were in full agreement and were therefore *at one* with each other, then all was well. But when these differences culminate to a highly contentious level, the various churches end up divorcing themselves from each other. This divergence of strong opinion is called a "schism", which is a legal term in church law for the formal separation of the church into two or more critical doctrinal opinions. One very notable schism dates back hundreds of years to the Reformation era.

The Reformation

Hundreds of years ago when certain members of the Catholic church hierarchy were making some very bad decisions, those decisions began to cause division within the church. This continued to build tensions within the church until people began to push back against these wrongs that were occurring at the hand of church leaders. One such person was Martin Luther. For those who are younger and who are reading this, Martin Luther was a German-Catholic studying to be a priest who lived hundreds of years ago, not to be confused with Dr. Martin Luther King Jr. who lived during the mid-nineteen-hundreds who fought for equal rights for those who were of African descent.

Martin Luther, the German-Catholic, studied to be a Catholic priest, but upon his contemplation of the weight of the vocation that he was undertaking, Martin began to doubt his own worthiness. He also began to question the direction that the church hierarchy was taking the church. The Pope at that time approved the selling of "indulgences". These "indulgences" were basically said to be able to save loved ones or one's own self from going to hell. Indulgences were in truth a fund-raising effort to build a new cathedral. The idea of selling indulgences utterly invalidates God's gift of Salvation done through the Pure Blood of The Christ. If indulgences were true and from God it would invalidate Christ's death causing the whole point of everything that God did to bring about the Salvation of mankind through Christ to be rendered worthless.

So, Martin Luther penned what we today call his "Ninety-Five Theses" or ninety-five points of error in doctrine. Martin nailed his theses to the door of the Wittenberg Castle church in Germany. You can read a bit more about this part of the Reformation in the book *Understanding The Bible*. Martin Luther's rebellion in this matter did not sit well with many church leaders who were profiting from the sales of indulgences. Amidst the ups and downs of the Luther saga, the church pushed back against Martin in a very strong way, but there were many people who agreed with Martin, or at least they did not agree with the church regarding indulgences being sold and other such matters that were important to them. This all caused a chasm to develop between the Catholic church hierarchy, and those who did not like the direction that the Catholic church was heading. This all came to a boiling point and the rebellion became violent and prominent.

The Catholic church tried to have Martin recant his public statements, but at his refusal the church tried to silence him. This all added to the tensions between sides in this saga. These rebels where fighting against the church hierarchy in effort to reform the church and bring it back in to alignment with Truth.

Make no mistake about it, there was enough arrogance on all sides of this fight to inflame the situation to a schismatic point of combustion. As Martin was cast off by the Catholic church, he continued in his quest to reform the church, but it caused unexpected consequences. There is a great deal more to this story, of which some additional key points are discussed in *Understanding The Bible*. Those who followed Martin Luther were derogatorily referred to as "Lutherans"–and it stuck. Martin did not intend to divide the Catholic church in this way. He was at one time a devout Catholic and actually died a devout Catholic in his heart. He wanted to follow the Bible as best he understood it. In fact, Martin played a role in the German translation of the Bible. He believed, as most Christians do, that Salvation cannot be bought with money as was wrongly implied through the idea of buying indulgences. Rather, Salvation comes only through our understanding that the only way to cleanse us from the Original Sin is by accepting Salvation through the Blood of The Christ by *knowing* that Christ is the Promised Savior, that is to say by True Faith.

He's Mine! No! He's Mine!

Over time the label "Lutheran" stuck, causing that side of the schism to eventually form itself into its own church sect. Now, inherent in rebellion is the gene that will pass itself along in the doctrine of the rebellion. With the Lutherans that gene is the disdain for the Catholic corruption that Martin Luther had towards the hierarchy of the Catholic church of his time. The gene of rebellion has been passed down from generation to generation to this very day in most other universal sects that arose from this conflict.

The gene is *rebellion* and it has infected each division that descended from the Luther rebellion. While what Martin said was true, the unintended consequences of this rebellion were certainly not expected by him at that time. Martin did not want to break up the church—he wanted to *change* it. We might question his techniques, but we have to understand that he was fighting a losing battle. In the history that follows Martin's actions, you will see this rebellion gene cause division upon division within the protesting-wings of Christianity. The Catholic church has largely stayed in unity over the centuries when compared with the constantly occurring schisms in the protesting church wings. These protesting sects create evermore new religions, with each new church or religion claiming superiority of alliance with God, insisting that their way is **the** way, as if somehow we humans can dictate to God what is true or not true.

These churches are much like hostile women fighting over a man. "He's Mine! No, He's Mine! No, He's Mine!" It's several unkempt women fighting over a man who is repulsed by every one of them. These fighting hostile women are far different from one complete and beautiful bride who freely and wholly offers her whole self to her groom. She makes herself beautiful for him and flirts with him and entices him to court her and then she eventually invites him into her wholly and completely. This is not so with the churches at the turn of the twentieth century.

The Upside of Division

Since the schism of Reformation has occurred and has birthed many more schisms, we have to deal with it and find the upside in this saga. One upside is—*the proving of other ideas*—through disagreement. The bystanders who are the congregants in these fractured churches should take advantage of this and evaluate what each church says, and then consider the arguments that each group or sect makes about any differences between sides. Many truths are exposed when we drop our biases and examine the information and circumstances with open hearts and open minds while seeking only Truth.

It is noteworthy that the primary religion was Catholic and that the Lutherans and those in the church of England were all Catholic prior to the Reformation era. This is a critical point for people of all religions, especially Christian religions, to understand if we want to truly *Understand The Church*. These various groups did not spontaneously form, they all descended from the Catholic faith and are largely in agreement, and all recognize similar and even identical creeds and prayers. All of Christendom came from what we now call the Catholic church. While we discussed "indulgences" being a critical cause of the Reformation schism, we did not discuss the gateway that allowed so many errors in our thinking, thus enabling us to create such problems.

Saul-Paul

The Paul person who is mentioned in the Bible and who is responsible for several of the New Testament epistles is referred to as the "apostle Paul", but he actually was not one of Jesus' twelve Apostles. Only eleven Apostles remained after Judas Iscariot ended himself for his betrayal of Christ. An apostle forges a path in a new area and is a follower of a leader who instructs. So Paul can technically be called an apostle, but in the context of the Bible, doing so confuses the issue.

This false apostle is called Paul, but Saul was his name and he sought to kill and defeat anyone who would follow or promote the teachings of Jesus The Christ. Saul hated Christ's followers. Saul was Pharisee. Saul claims to have had an appearance of some sort where, in a blinding light, allegedly The Christ spoke to him and asked Saul why he was persecuting The Christ. This encounter changed Saul, and Saul now called himself Paul. No reason is given for this name change.

After this encounter, Saul, who was now called Paul, would go out and preach to people about Jesus. Saul-Paul was a Pharisee. Pharisees are legalistic about law like lawyers are, and they arrogantly nitpick to accuse both the guilty and innocent alike. Being a legalistic Pharisee was in Saul-Paul's nature and he never really got beyond it as he traveled while teaching the news about The Christ. Now there are those who completely disregard Paul, but most people in the church dwell on Paul's words a bit too much. In fact, while this will be denied by most churches, it is true nonetheless; most churches are based more upon Saul-Paul than they are Peter who they claim is the rock of their church.

Saul-Paul's words are the sand foundation upon which almost every Christian church today has chosen to build itself. It's not that Saul-Paul is altogether wrong, but rather that his words are taken as "Gospel" when in fact they are *not* Gospel. Saul-Paul was little more than a typical preacher of our modern era and he never actually knew Jesus The Christ. Except for his own account of his encounter with the blinding light, there is no evidence of any interaction between him and The Christ. The true Apostles knew Jesus The Christ personally, and they were often together with him and ate with him and traveled with him. They were Christ's close personal friends.

This faulty Pauline sand foundation that most churches have been building themselves upon is often in conflict with the teachings of the actual Christ. Or at minimum *people's interpretations* of some of Saul-Paul's teachings are in conflict with Christ's teachings. If you look into this even a little bit with a clear unbiased and open mind, seeking only Truth, you will quickly see the error in this and that is it prevalent in nearly all Christian religious sects.

How can we test this hypothesis? If you were to pull out all of the church Doctrine that is based upon Saul-Paul's statements that are included in the *Catechism of the Catholic Church*, the book would greatly diminish in size, and the Catholic church as understood by many would collapse. We can actually witness the implosion of the church even without removing the Pauline doctrine. The fractures that are allowed due to the adherence Saul-Paul's writings are what allow much of the dissension within the churches. The Jewish Pharisaical ways of Saul-Paul are borne into the church and, good or not, they have been causing division for centuries. Saul did not believe that Jesus was the prophesied Messiah, and Saul persecuted Christ's followers until he had his blinding encounter. We must not forget Saul-Paul's origins when trying to understand him or his writings.

Saul-Paul carries so much weight with most churches that they make him out to be equal to the Apostles and even superior to them in authority. But, while Saul-Paul is often referred to as an "apostle", he was not one of the twelve and never will be. The twelfth Apostle position was vacated by Judas Iscariot after he betrayed Christ and then ended himself. The position was subsequently filled sometime after Christ's death and Resurrection and it appears that it was shortly after his Ascension. The eleven remaining true Apostles had two equally good candidates to replace Judas Iscariot, whose names are: *Joseph Barsabbas Justus* and also *Matthias*. They gave the two men lots and the lot fell to Matthias. So Matthias then took the position of the twelfth Apostle. It was **not** and is **not** Saul-Paul the Pharisee, as many people tend to subconsciously assume.

Peter

We should take issue with any church that places Saul-Paul's words before Peter's words, that is to say, Peter who was appointed to be the rock on which Christ would establish his Church. Most of us have an incorrect thought that only those mentioned by name in the Bible taught about Christ, but Christ told some of those who He encountered that were believers that they should go out and preach to others ahead of him.

But regarding Saul-Paul, it is error to establish any church upon Saul-Paul's writings. Simon-Peter is that rock and just because a church claims to be built upon Peter does not mean that that church is built upon Peter. If it walks like Saul-Paul and talks like Saul-Paul, it is of Saul-Paul.

A True Church will dwell on the Words of Christ over those of Saul-Paul, but this practice is frighteningly absent from most churches. The Vatican is said to be the seat of the church with authority handed from one Pope to the next all the way back to Peter the foundation of Rock. This may be so, but if that church diverges from Christ's teachings and Peter's guidance, and replaces it with Saul-Paul's teachings or any other teaching instead, then there will be problems. So while the foundation might be solid and immovable, that does not mean that the church that has been built upon it is well-built.

The Vatican has had its ups and downs, such as those spoken of in the section about Martin Luther and the Reformation. But to its credit, the Catholic church has been in place for a very long time. Rare, but every so many years, usually centuries, adjustments will be made to attempt to correct doctrine with new revelations that might not have been known or properly understood regarding Catholic doctrine. One such major shift was the inception of Vatican II.

Vatican II

Let's first investigate the word itself, "Vatican". *Vatican* or *Vatic* at its root can be *prophet, poet,* or even *mad*–like *crazy* or insane. While at times we do see somewhat insane behavior coming out of the Vatican, such as that exhibited early in the twenty-first century, here we will consider the Vatican over its entirety to get a more rational point of observation. In general, the Popes have been reasonably good, at least outwardly. And some of them have spoken and taught some very compelling ideas. Any truly good Pope will guide the church towards Truth. Thus if a good Pope sees error in the church doctrine, then that Pope will work towards the goal of adjusting that erred doctrine and make that information open to scrutiny, and eventually it will be implemented into the teachings of the Catholic church.

In science and medicine many terms are coined using the Latin or Greek languages due to the fact that those languages are generally no longer used and thus do not get contaminated with the perversion of contemporary language as the years progress. These languages remain stable and thus are suitable in scientific fields due to their stabile unchanging nature when we need to accurately pass information to successive generations.

The church said everything in the Latin language for many years, including creating copies of the Bible painstakingly transcribed and eventually block printed. The Liturgy was also said in Latin even though the congregation around the world did not know the "Sacred Latin" language.

When the Gutenberg printing press was invented, the first book printed on it was a Vulgate Bible version partly in Latin and partly in Greek language. Martin Luther also wanted to bring the Bible's words to the people in the people's native language, and after being cast out of the assembly he sought to translate the Bible into his native German language.

A part of Vatican II was to allow Liturgy to be said in the people's native languages and also for the priest to face the people while doing mass. But Vatican II also loosened church rules on other aspects of teachings, some of which caused rifts and contributed to the potential slow demise of the Catholic church. But a big part of the problem with Vatican II is more like with Martin Luther, in that when the change occurs, those changes are often misunderstood and thus abused by people. Vatican II was to be a kinder and gentler church that would be more open and more inviting. That option sounds good on the surface, but that change inserted a brand-new gene into the Catholic church's DNA, but this time the gene is not separated out like it was with Martin Luther. This time the gene is grafted directly into the Catholic church. What is that gene? It is the gene of easing of teachings and rules.

SSPX

Rules are good. Rules are guidelines that we use to tread as we navigate life, but at times many rules are authoritarian. In others words, "Shut up and do as I say". Jesus The Christ was not so pushy in that way, instead he made basic statements of Truth and he stood by them. Christ was not going to punish us, we would do that of our own accord by not heeding his alerts. I would call them "warnings" but some people could take that as more threatening. Christ made statements of fact. Christ was not going to decide your fate. Your fate is up to you through your choices. To become more accepting of people and more understandable to people, Vatican II was implemented, but it was done with great pushback by many people and parishes. Yes, it is good if we seek to be more Christ-like if we are in fact being more Christ-like.

After several years of dissatisfaction with the changes of Vatican II, those who pushed back against Vatican II formed the Society of Saint Pius X (the SSPX) founded by a French Archbishop, Marcel Lefebvre. This movement sought to return to the original Vatican doctrine. It slowly gained ground over the years, but SSPX had not gained adequate traction in order to really get the movement going. The SSPX believed that the Pope's chair has been vacant ever since Vatican II was officially established in 1965. We might assume that SSPX has failed, but when it comes to matters of religion we must think in terms of centuries rather than decades. However, the SSPX is not without its own problems.

FSSP

The FSSP, yet another fracture in the Catholic church, much like SSPX, is the Priestly Fraternity of Saint Peter which broke off from the SSPX. It is a bit more in line with the Vatican due to its recognition of the Pope, but it too has rejected aspects of Vatican II, and its adherents also perform the ancient Roman Liturgy in Latin. These fractures in the Catholic church are the result of Vatican II, and these petty differences between sects have little to do with the True Church of Christ. The differences have to do with man's rules and man's failed interpretation of the Bible. But in all of our foolish human ways we must remember that The Christ said, "If they are not against us they are for us."

However, this is not just people going about their own way. In some cases, there's conflict between the various factions, thus whether a sect is still called Catholic or if it is of the protestant wing of Christianity, then "If they are not for us they are against us."

No one will get me to believe that this infighting is what Christ wanted of his True Church. As a matter of fact, any person or group/sect that breaks away from Christ's Words is well on the way to stepping across the threshold as they leave the True Church of Christ.

Modern Pharisees

The Pharisees of the time of Christ were legalistic authoritarians who would not abide by their own interpretation of the laws of the Torah, yet they sought to impose their own interpretation of those same laws onto the people, which might sound familiar to you with regard to modern government. While the Pharisees were not specifically the governing body of the land, they did hold considerable sway over the church in those days.

History has witnessed this same legalistic authoritarianism many times over the years. For instance, during Galileo Galilei's time, Galileo looked to the heavens with the newly invented telescope and reasoned that the Earth was not the center point of everything and that the Sun did not go around the Earth, but rather that the Earth revolved around the Sun. For this he was silenced and was expected to recant his findings. The scientific leaders or scientists in the Catholic church at that time would not have it; they were incapable of allowing their minds to open up to the truth that Galileo had uncovered.

We see this same thing today, but today it's outside of the Church. At one point in history, the Church was the primary supporter of science, but this began to change after the suppression and scandal surrounding Galileo's findings. This diverging of science at that time was proper because we are to learn and to find Truth. If a church will not allow investigation to seek Truth, then that church is not to be trusted. Sadly, this schism between the church and science, versus Truth continues to this day, but the church and science have now become two completely separate religions. The temples of science are now where great tales are told unlike anything before them. Somehow, in the time from Galileo to the modern era, science has gone from seeking Truth to forbidding it, and its priests and pharisees are the professors and scientists who promote its doctrine of lies and its inaccuracies.

Today we have our modern pharisees in both the universal churches and in the church of science, and it appears that no matter what we seek, we will be ridiculed for revealing any glimmer of Truth. If you doubt this, simply question some of these pharisees about "climate change", or evolution, or the validity and authority of Saul-Paul's teachings, you will quickly feel the crushing hand of their respective religion crashing down upon you. And if you get public about it they, will attempt to publicly destroy your reputation so that other people will not take you seriously for their own fear of getting caught in the muck and mire that these pharisees are throwing at you.

Sabbath Day

To jump topics briefly here, why is the "Sabbath" day considered special? And is Sunday the Sabbath day? In the first chapter of Genesis, God worked on Creation for six days and then on the seventh day God rested. We were instructed by God to do likewise. In Hebrew the number seven is pronounced Shabbat. Even our word seven is derived from that. In the Hebrew language the letter "b" can make either the *b* or *v* sound. The vowels have been translated in various ways due to differing dialects, but most prominent languages of the western world all use something close enough to be recognized as a direct derivative of "Sabbath"—so, *sbn* or *svn*. You can see the sounds of two of the prominent letters at work here.

Translation is a tricky bit of work, and decoding it is often more difficult because you must first understand and know the origins of the individual person who translated the text you intend to study. In any case, "Sabbath" means *seven*. God rested on the Sabbath meaning that God rested on what to us is the seventh day, and thus the seventh day is the Sabbath. For those who lived during, or have talked with or read about people prior to the nineteen-seventies, you might recall a time when many stores were closed on weekends. And while we went to church on Sunday and thought that it was the Sabbath, we were wrong. In past times Saturday was a day of rest and lounging. Saturday was a day to be with family and relax and enjoy. Saturday is the seventh day on most calendars, and it is the day of rest in which to look back and enjoy the fruits of your work.

The Catholic church has been the keeper of the calendar, but through turbulent times and the ebb and flow of the church, the church has not been able to perfect the calendar. Few people realize or care about this, but the calendar is not perfectly accurate. Sure, when we are talking thousands of years it's pretty much on track, but to know certain specific dates as per the more accurate calendar of stars in the heavens, we simply do not know. Our modern calendar is close, but it is off. There are a few things we do have correct. A day is a day and a year is a year and Baby Jesus was born roughly a couple of thousand years ago. And we have the days of the week right, we just misunderstand them.

Some of the discrepancies in our understanding of the calendar were induced by rejection of culture. For instance, the Jews and Christians distanced themselves from one another due to the schism that occurred because of The Christ. We must keep in mind that the Jews and the rest of Israel are from the same root as Christ's True Church, because before Christ came they all believed same things, that is until Christ died and rose from the dead and Ascended into Heaven. At that point, for whatever reason, many of the Jews, especially the hierarchy, refused to accept Jesus The Christ as the long-awaited Messiah.

This division of groups caused irrational rejection of certain doctrines and traditions by each other and thus Sunday became the Sabbath to Christians even though Saturday is still the seventh day of the week on most calendars, especially Christian calendars. After Christ came it was no longer one large single collective people who followed the Mosaic ways, instead there was now a division between those who accepted Christ as the Promised Savior, versus those who rejected Christ as the Promised Savior.

But, while not all things were abandoned by Christians, us believing that the Sabbath is Sunday is really our own fault for not paying attention. It's also our own fault for not paying attention that we don't realize that certain holiday traditions are mistakenly celebrated per the phases of the moon, a practice that we have stuck to for over twenty-five hundred years. Using the moon as the basis for any annual church celebration date is really quite absurd. Moon calculated holy days cause these holidays to at times to be celebrated weeks apart depending upon where you are located on the globe. Celebrating weeks apart is not being at one with each other. The seventh day was to be a day of rest, a holy or whole day of joy—Temple services would then follow. And all Christian holidays should be celebrated based upon Earth's position relative to the stars and our Sun so that we celebrate them as one or "at one" with each other all around the world.

What people who want to be a part of Christ's True Church must come to understand is that to be in unity we must follow Christ's Words, rather than man's rules. And we must realize that many leaders in the various churches use inconsistent and inaccurate doctrine that follows Saul-Paul, rather than following The Christ or Peter. This will be argued by these groups because most of them speak about what Saul-Paul said about Christ, but here in this statement is their flaw revealed.

Circumcision

Part of the longstanding Mosaic laws (The Laws given to Moses as the Israelites left Egypt) was that all of the male Israelites were to be circumcised by having the foreskin of the penis removed when they were yet babies just a few days after they were born. And anyone that was to join with the Israelites was to become like them and adopt their culture and those who were males were to be circumcised. This was a very personal way to mark them all as "Israelites". In our modern era, some people frown upon circumcision and call it "genital mutilation" and then turn and tattoo themselves with lifelong permanent markings or, even worse, they will remove the penis altogether, or for some women the breasts will be removed. The irony in such bodily mutilation is really quite astounding to behold. Circumcision was done very early on in the Bible and was a way of symbolizing that you were of God's People, but nay, in recent times this too has been ridiculed and rejected while other bodily mutilations far worse are being done.

Longstanding truths are ever increasingly rejected by modern cultures as we forget our true roots. The Hebrew circumcision that marked the people as "God's People" is now rejected by many unknowing people who have fallen prey to the societal lies and incorrect analysis of information. Circumcision was debated by people in the epistles because they were failing to understand who specifically it was that was supposed to be circumcised. Circumcision was not for the entire world, but Salvation is, and the two are not related or connected in any way as pertaining to Salvation.

The Council of Trent

Jumping forward again in time for a moment to Martin Luther and the Reformation, the Council of Trent was assembled as a sort of response to the Reformation movement. The council sought to clarify the core Catholic belief as if the Nicaean creed was insufficient. During this council, specific statements of doctrine were then established in the older Catholic book titled *"Council of Trent Catechism for the Parishes"* first penned in the mid fifteen-hundreds. This is where the Catholic church codified the fact that it was the church of Saul-Paul rather than Christ's True Church founded on Simon-Peter. Of course, if taken to task on this point it will be vehemently denied by the Catholic church. But read the Trent Catechism for yourself and count the Saul-Paul quotes and derivatives thereof, versus those of Simon-Peter and of Christ—you will be shocked!

In the modern Catechism of the Catholic church this is a bit more difficult to discern because the Pauline references are relegated to citation numbers that you must look up in the index in order to tell where they are quoted from, and even then, it is somewhat obscure. And even more ambiguous, Saul-Paul's quotes are often not shown at all and are only referenced by arbitrary sequential numbers, they are then replaced with a modern interpretation of Saul-Paul's words which is mostly done through maybe a short quote with the larger part of the text being someone else's thoughts on Saul-Paul's words. This means that the Catechism is third- and fourth-hand information rather than the first-hand accounts read in the Gospels. Unless someone is very Bible-savvy, which is rare indeed, you will not be able to readily tell what text comes *from what or who* in the modern versions of the *"Catechism of the Catholic Church"*.

In many ways it is a good thing that the church worked to codify the doctrine in the Catechism books because when we write things down in a tangible manner, as opposed to just saying them from memory or even putting them in electronic form for public view, they cannot be changed once printed. "It is Written" is a very important statement. When something is written and then rewritten at a later date, there is then evidence of any changes having taken place. Without words being written down, future generations would have no indication regarding any changes or errors that may have crept into their current doctrinal information. It is time for those who seek to be a part of Christ's True Church to awaken and see all there is to see. There are many good things to rediscover and many incorrect doctrinal traditions that need to be cleaned up a bit.

God is On Our Side

If you think about this, you will likely recall people over the years within any given religion during times of debate and tension stating that "God is on our side". It may in fact be so that they and God happen to be on the same side, but God doesn't choose sides. God is immovable. God states something so and it is so, this does not mean that God doesn't ever change direction. God has softened many times when wrath was due, but because of the pleading prayers of faithful servants, God was merciful and gave people second and third chances.

But, God has set rules in place that not even the pleading of the saints will alter, yet God will soften wrath that is about to descend upon evil doers because of the prayers the righteous. These immovable rules are our guidelines for good living. When we live by these guidelines *we choose* to be on God's side rather than foolishly believing that God has chosen our side.

God does not "choose sides". God is God, and we choose to be with God or against God. That choice, as a church and as an individual, is ours to make through our freewill. Will you choose to be on God's side, or on man's side?

Chapter 8

Building a Temple of God

What we have discussed so far is that Christ's True Church is to be established upon the solid foundational rock of Simon-Peter. We also discussed that the Church was originally intended to stay established upon Peter, but was eventually shifted over to quietly become the church of Saul-Paul. Christ said that he would tear down the temple and build it up again in three days. And since Christ embodied the very Spirit of God, it was He who was the True "Temple of God". That's all simple enough to understand, but where things get confusing to us is in the transition from *temple* to *church*

In our modern English Bibles, it says that Christ would establish his "Church" upon Simon-Peter. He didn't say temple, he said Church. Let's investigate this briefly: What was the first temple? A temple is like a womb where we are to be nurtured and cared for through the passing along of information.

The Tent of Meeting

The very first temples were often outside on a rock where offerings were made to God, such as where Abraham was going to offer Isaac as sacrifice at the request of God in order to test Abraham, but that was only a test for Abraham to see if he loved God above all else, so God stopped Abraham and exchanged his son for a ram caught in the thicket to be used for the offering. Making offerings goes way, way back to Adam. When Adam was severely injured by Satan, Adam took some grass and wiped up his own blood and offered it up to God. God was very pleased with this gesture of soul and promised Adam that when The Word was to come through the righteous seed of Adam that He would offer His own blood for the Salvation of Adam and Eve and their righteous offspring.

This tradition of offering sacrifices as Adam did was carried through thousands of years, even up to the time of the Israelites' Exodus from Egypt. As they left Egypt and whined and complained, they were forced to wander in the desert for forty years. This occurred because God was angry with them because after God having performed the Bible's most stunning miracles, the Israelites rejected and doubted God and they wanted to go back to the same Egypt that they previously had constantly complained about and prayed for deliverance from. During that time of wandering in the desert, they sought a centralized place where God could dwell with them in which they could make sacrificial offerings to God, they were then instructed to make a portable tent or tabernacle.

They were also instructed to build a small Ark, not Noah's ark, but a much smaller and very elaborate Ark to hold certain important things that were given them during their desert wandering period. Among these possessions were the five books of the Torah given to Moses, along with the Ten Commandments and some other important items. These five Torah books were likely written on leather or animal skins. They were kept safely in the Ark which was kept in the elaborate tabernacle tent that they made.

The Levite Priests would go into this tent into the innermost parts almost like a womb within the tent and offer up bread and flesh. God would then consume these offerings with fire if they were found acceptable. These traditions were carried on for many years after.

The Temple

When the years of wandering in the desert finally ended, the Israelites quickly decided that they needed a King to lead them. God did not want this, but they insisted. God wanted them to self-govern. Saul, not Saul-Paul, but a different Saul much earlier in the timeline, was to be anointed king. But as humanity would have it, King Saul failed as a suitable leader and was to be replaced: Saul's replacement was to be little David, the very same David who slew Goliath the giant. There's a whole story behind the contention that occurs between David and King Saul that we won't elaborate on here, but eventually David did become king. After David was king for a time, he had a child named Solomon, the details of which we also will not elaborate on here.

Since Israel wandered in the desert for so long, assembling and disassembling the tent, David wanted to build a special stationary temple now that they were settled in one place. However, God did not want David to build the temple because David was a warrior and had blood on his hands, but God told David that his son could build the temple. So instead, David collected vast materials in preparation for the building of the temple.

King David's son, Solomon, did build the temple using the materials his father David had accumulated for the project, this temple is often referred to as "Solomon's Temple". This was a grand undertaking, and based upon the description of the temple that you read in the Bible, it was quite an amazing structure.

They offered sacrifices in the temple, but it is important to note that a "Temple" is a place of observation and is rooted in the word "Tome" which is basically a roll of papyrus. That is to say that the temple is the place to observe what is written on the papyrus, which was the Torah—the first five books of the Bible.

The True Temple

Solomon's temple was truly a grand Temple that took years to construct by many people dedicated fulltime to the task. Just to tear down such a temple would be many months of work. The Temple, as mentioned in the last section, is a place of observation of the words of God. This should make it clear that it is we who are the True temple of God. And when we accept the Blood of The Christ and the Sacrifice of Christ into our hearts, then The Word of God dwells within us. This is why God insists that we purify ourselves with the Pure Blood of the Lamb of God. Do we want to invite God into our home if our home is filthy? Or are we going to keep our home clean so that when God enters into us we are prepared and ready for God to dwell within us?

It is no mistake that the Husband and Wife are always used as an analogy of our relationship to God. This is obvious when you remember and understand that we are made in the image of God. Imagine being a man and your wife is filthy after she has been with other men to a point where she is diseased. Is this inviting to you? Would you want to enter into her? Probably not. And let's reverse the situation. If a wife is pure and clean and ready, will she want her husband to have been with other women and him carrying disease from them? Probably not. If you ponder these things along this line of thinking you should, if you have not yet, be able to form pretty clear connections helping you to understand the need for purity within the Church, as well as within our earthly marriages and in our own hearts, minds, and earthly bodies.

The Temple of Christ

It is clear that we are all pure temples of The Word of God when we are clean and prepared like a bride is on her wedding day as we allow God into us. But there is a more perfect temple in Jesus The Christ. Christ, who is The Word made Flesh, became the Fullness of the Temple of God. When Christ spoke with the Pharisees and said to them "Tear down this temple and I will rebuild in it three days", they assumed The Christ spoke of Solomon's grand Temple, but Christ was speaking of when The Word was Made Flesh it was part of God fulfilling the promise to Adam and Eve, and if they killed Him, He would be rebuilt or Resurrected within only three days.

Mistaken Identity

When the Israelites left Egypt they were known as "God's People". And it is those people that are chronicled in the Bible. What is so special about these people that *their* history was recorded in such an articulate manner over so many years? Actually, nothing is special about them. In fact, they have repeatedly fallen short of the expectations that God had of them. They lied, cheated, stole, raped, plundered, murdered, worshipped idols, and the list goes on and on. The Israelites as a whole group have never been particularly special.

So what is it that caused them to be called "God's Chosen People"? It's all about promises made. The original covenant was with Adam and Eve where God promised to send The Word and The Word would be made flesh through one of Adam's righteous offspring. This same Promise was continued through many other people, but namely through Noah, then Abraham and then through Isaac, and then through *Jacob* who at one point God renamed "*Israel*". God made a Promise that through these people's offspring, the Promise made to Adam and Eve would be fulfilled. And that is what is so special about them; they were the genealogical trail to The Christ that God chose because some key people in that lineage were wholly dedicated to God, and it is through them that the Promise was carried.

Many People who are thought to not be direct descendants of the Israelites feel left out because they are not considered to be a part of "God's Chosen People". But we must remember the things written in the Bible about outsiders coming into the congregation. The people coming in were to adopt the practices of the Israelites and abide by the standards set forth by God. Thus, everyone is welcome when they follow those simple guidelines.

Further, just because you are not one of "God's Chosen People" by genealogical blood relation does not mean that you cannot be saved as many people often wrongly believe. This confusion even troubled the Apostles and it was debated by them as told in the book of Acts. The Promise to Adam and Eve **applies to all of mankind**, but The Word Made Flesh would come through only one specific lineage as that person could not occur through every lineage of man. The lineage was chosen due to the dedication of certain individuals along the way and came through the lineage of those who were most dedicated to God. That is to say that when one man or woman was wholly dedicated to God in the lineage as it unfolded, then the promise would go through the dedicated person's family of that time.

God's Chosen People versus the Church

Christ's Church, which was to be established upon Simon-Peter, is often incorrectly recognized as "God's People", and while this is partly true, it falls short, very short, of reality. Where does this proprietary notion come from? A part of it inadvertently comes directly from God. God wanted the people to remain pure and thus stay away from the heathen sinners. But that's not God's problem, it is mankind's problem—it is our problem. God wants any of those who choose God, to be pure, but purity does not occur when we are comingling with sinners who have decided to *not* repent of their sins and who refuse to stop sinning. Many non-Christian people attempt to emulate the God-to-man relationship through other means, such as human sacrifice and serving other "gods" and idols. But this perversion of reality only serves to upset the actual Creator God. This misunderstood serving of other gods causes an ever-increasing rift between those people and God. However, it is the Israelites' *duty* to share Truth with the world. But non-Israelites do not carry that same burden, yet they are welcomed to help. So when people convert to Christianity there is an incorrect assumption that they have become one of God's "Chosen People". The Chosen people is a blood line and has nothing to do with anyone's Salvation other than that the Savior of all of mankind was born through that bloodline.

When the Israelites were wandering through the desert and when they were establishing themselves in their new-found homeland, they were commissioned to teach others their ways, rather than others teaching the Israelites the ways of the heathen. Then, later on when Christ dubbed Simon the *petra* or *pater*, that is to say the *Father* or **rock**, he was in a way given the keys to Christ's Church as is symbolically represented in the statue art of the "Consignment to Peter" depicted on the cover of this book.

Jesus sent out seventy of his followers to the areas that he would soon visit. These areas were likely areas of descendants of the Israelites. Jesus also instructed his twelve Apostles to go out and teach. They were to spread this Good news to the "Jews" first and then the rest of the Israelite tribes and then to the Gentiles. Since the Israelites were "God's Chosen People" they were basically the first in line for the Promise of Salvation and also because they were the ones who were entrusted to spread the message of the Good news throughout the world.

But Christ's Church is not so small that it is unable to contain more than only the Israelites. If you think back to the promise God made to Adam and Eve, God promised that through their

Righteous seed God would send The Word and that Word would become flesh and be the Salvation for **any** of Adam and Eve's **righteous** offspring. Thus, the True Church is to be made up of all of man who abide by the simple guidelines set forth by God and The Christ, and we also must fully-of-heart accept and believe that The Christ was The Word of God come to save man. It is Simple and free!

Now, when you consider the chain of events surrounding this family of people through whom the Promise would be bestowed, you will quickly find that it was narrowed down considerably at the time of Noah's flood when only eight souls remained. The Promise went through Noah and his family. But remember that Noah and his family were obviously descendants of Adam and Eve, and we today are also descendants of Adam and Eve—all of us, all of the world. The promise of Salvation through the Christ *is for **all** of man* and was to be taught to all of man through the Israelites. There is no need for false gods or human sacrifice or any other unusual practices. **All** people are invited into the Kingdom and need only abide by a few basic and somewhat obvious guidelines.

Chapter 9

The Church of Self

When you consider all of the small signs that God did in regard to prophecy, and that Christ took on himself many similar things that happened to Adam, it gets pretty difficult to rationally deny that Jesus The Christ is, in fact, The Christ who is the long-awaited Savior/Redeemer/Messiah. And further, when you study even a little bit about anthropology, you will quickly see who "God's People" are. It is quite notably visible in most aspects of the culture of God's People because you see it in their worship, and in their everyday-behavior, and their everyday-language. But as for Christ's True Church, that it is quite a different story.

Most "Christians", and most non-Christians for that matter, are more attentive to the church-of-self than we are to the Church of Christ. Our self-centered way of life blinds us from the path we ought to be on, thus causing us to veer wildly off course. When observing our self-centered–church-of-self, you can witness the wreckage from our errors strewn about nearly everywhere you look. Being in Christ's Church comes with long-term benefits that help us avoid becoming a part of that wreckage.

Protect Yourself from Evil

It sounds simple right? Just protect yourself from evil! While this sounds simple, the reality is that we live in Satan's world. Satan is the master of this lower world and our flesh is subject to the lures of Satan. We all still must die as per the Original Sin violation and man's submission to Satan in the Garden of Eden. This world can be a wonderful place when we rebel against the lures of Satan and choose to be on God's side. But when we collectively inch ourselves away from God, and society as a whole adopts destructive and very peculiarly unsavory behavior, then choosing to be on God's side comes at a cost. For when you choose to be on God's side, the world will stand against you and ridicule you and torment you, sometimes even unto death. But when society collectively chooses to be on God's side and follows the ways of Christ, then we live in peace and harmony, joy and prosperity, free of most disease and torment.

It was made quite clear that we were to protect ourselves from evil as is indicated in The Lord's Prayer when Jesus said "lead us not into temptation but deliver us from evil." Within that statement is the underlying idea that we are to stay clear of bad things and will likely need God's assistance in doing so.

For a Bag of Silver

Evil is so predominant in our human nature that we are often willing to betray even The Christ himself. As another one of God's markers regarding who the person of The Christ is, was the marker of Judas Iscariot who betrayed Jesus for money when he was paid to deliver Christ to the soldiers with the sign of a kiss. A kiss is a very personal sign of love, and to be betrayed using a kiss made that particular betrayal event an even more astoundingly severe violation.

It's easy for those who live now or have lived these many years later after Judas betrayed Christ, to judge Judas and think, "Well, I would never do that to Jesus", or "How could someone do that to Jesus?" But, betrayals lurk almost everywhere around us. While you yourself might have high enough integrity to not betray Truth in the way that Judas Iscariot did, this is not so with everyone. Just consider the lies vomited forth by the news media in the early part of the twenty-first century. Will we somehow imagine that they had good intentions behind all of their lies and suppression of Truth? No, these people have sold both their souls and their fellow man out for the price of money, and being the useful fools that they are, they did so at bargain prices.

These children of Satan lie and cheat and steal and defame every single day for nothing more than their status. Sure, they like the millions of dollars that many of them are paid to do so, but it is more important to them that they receive the accolades of their peers and that they "get the story". This is true even though most of those stories are tainted with outright lies or suppressed details that deliberately cause those stories to be improperly understood by the audience, and thus are utterly dishonest reports.

Always remember that betrayal is common and it will likely happen to you at some point in your life. You must work very diligently in protecting yourself from doing it to others, and if possible from others doing it to you.

Protect Yourself from Yourself

If any one of us hopes to ever be a True member of the True Church of Christ, then we must protect ourselves from our worst enemy. That enemy is Satan, but our worst enemy can also be each our own self. When we fail to fill ourselves with the Holy Spirit of Truth, we can be assured that we will feel empty. Where there is a void, something will eventually fill it. You could think of this in terms of digging a deep hole with clean straight sides. If you immediately build a foundation in that hole after it is dug then the hole becomes filled with that foundation on which you can build your home. But if you fail to quickly establish that foundation, then eventually dirt will begin to fill in the hole as the dirt walls around it collapse into the hole.

Your person (yourself) is that hole, and if you fail to allow The Holy Spirit of Truth to establish itself as the foundation within that hole, then the filthy dirt that is all around you will fill that hole faster than you might expect.

When the void in us is filled with dirt, we then become our own worst enemy. People who are caught up in this are either blinded by the surrounding dirt or are too humiliated to seek help. At this point you must realize that God either exists, or God does not exist. If those who are not "believers" are correct, then nothing really matters and we can all go right on ahead and rape, rob, and plunder at will without moral consequence. However, if the believers are correct, then this all has *eternal* ramifications that will be a most unpleasant experience for those who do not believe and who refuse to repent. The unpleasant experience will make your worst day on Earth seem like the best day you have ever experienced in comparison. And to add to the matter, the torment you would experience will go on forever–that's *eternally!*

Only *you* can decide for yourself which road you will take. When you choose the wrong path you can blame it on Satan, but that won't stop the eternal torment that *you chose* of your own free will. This situation is confirmation in those cases that you were your own worst enemy if that happens to be the path you chose. The vast lies by the world that tell us that "religion is all bullshit", is perhaps the most heinous of lies. But from their clouded perspective, they do have a point. However, it is instead in regard to the incorrect perception of religion that most people have.

Embrace the Church

One very helpful way to protect yourself from the worst enemy being yourself, and from the source of your worst enemy which is Satan, is to embrace the True Church. Christ's True Church has been the saving Grace for countless humans over the centuries. When we lose focus on God and God's Truth we will almost always go wayward. This is why we so often see otherwise good people fall from Grace.

As mentioned in an earlier part of this book, the church on occasion ebbs and flows from good to corrupt. We expect church leaders to be true and righteous—we typically trust them. When however, they breach that trust, it is confusing to us. We were taught all of our lives that these priests were good and were good stewards of the congregation, but then a few, and yet far too many of them, corrupted themselves and yet still continue to be our "shepherds". To our minds this is confusing and illogical. Someone representing the ultimate good is doing the ultimate evil and calling it good. Have no doubt about it, these types of people have made themselves children of Satan and will abide in hell.

This is why in this book the Church is referred to as the True Church of Christ capitalizing the title. The True Church of Christ will embrace you and correct you. A false church will embrace you but will fail to correct you, and there is no form of evil greater than a leader's failure to guide, correct, and even discipline when needed. It is of no matter if that leader is a parent, a teacher, a politician, a prominent person, a preacher, or even a priest. If that shepherd fails to guide you to Truth, and instead guides you away from Truth, then they have done evil unto you.

Embrace the True Church of Christ and allow the Spirit of Truth to fill you until you are an overflowing fountain who can give others drink from the Truth now flowing out of you.

Chapter 10

The Commitment

When we embrace the True Church of Christ we become wed to Christ. It is a commitment made in front of the entire congregation as you take part in the Bread and Wine during Communion. When we violate that commitment we are divorcing ourselves as individuals from the Church body, and far worse, we are divorcing ourselves from The Christ Himself. Doing so is a one way ticket to eternal damnation. Please keep in mind that this is not referring to whether or not you *regularly* take communion, but rather that once you have taken communion then you have committed yourself to The Christ and if you violate your commitment then you are divorcing yourself from The Christ. However, God's longsuffering regarding our constant falling away allows us to repent more than once. But with this we must understand that it permanently tarnishes us a bit each time we fall away. When we do this repeatedly, it is like when a garment becomes permanently soiled through many exposures to filth. You can wash it and it will be clean, but it will no longer be pure and white. When you make the commitment, make the commitment and keep that promise for your best long-term results.

Hooked On Rules

It is inherent in man to seek answers, and much of that seeking is in regard to our life-guidance. Our desire for guidance and direction exists because we have a natural affinity to want to be guided toward God and to be with God and filled with God's Truth. Because we now live in a world that is controlled by Satan, the moment we lose sight of God we begin to become void and then the filth of the world immediately begins to slowly but constantly sift into us.

We feel this sin, this void, and seek to find direction. In order to assist us in our quest for direction, we set up societal guidelines. These guidelines are what we call "laws". But when we veer too far from the straight path, even these legal guidelines will fail us, thus leading us in a direction for which we are not prepared to cope. Any adult who has given even the slightest amount of attention to how laws are abused will be acutely aware of the damage that these abuses cause society. The Pharisees, or lawyers, of these laws take insignificant and well-intended stipulations placed in the laws and they turn those stipulations into loopholes that end up hanging us.

This obsession with rules is nothing new. It has infiltrated government time and time again over scores of hundreds of years, ultimately leading to societal collapse every time. Yet we seem to never learn from history as each newborn society repeats this same error as it ages.

Even the church gets in on this deceptive action. Earlier in this book the Saul-Paul epistles were discussed where this book implies that many of the ills of the world are caused due to Saul-Paul's epistle writings and/or misinterpretation thereof. Christ said "Ask and it will be given to you; seek and you will find; knock and the door will be opened to you. For everyone who asks receives; the one who seeks finds; and to the one who knocks, the door will be opened." If you seek this about Saul-Paul's writings you will find it. Now while most of Saul-Paul's epistles are worded in a peculiar manner, it is additionally often our own personal lying-interpretation of those epistles that causes us trouble. These troubles increase exponentially when the preaching "authorities" misinterpret these epistles and then relay their misinterpretation to us as if it was handed down directly from God, which it is not.

When law or doctrine is established it can help to guide us. But if the law or doctrine has too many caveats within, it can and will lead to misinterpretation. So again, the problem with Saul-Paul's epistles is not only Saul-Paul's convoluted words, but often it is our misinterpretation of those words. Before he became "Paul", he was Saul the *Pharisee*. Pharisees can be considered lawyers of their own doctrine which they derived from the Torah (those first five books of the Bible). If you have ever read case-law you will quickly come to understand how some lawyers can twist words to arrive at the loophole needed to achieve their legal desires and deceptions.

In patent and copyright law the objective is to keep things as simple and broad as possible. The more detail that is added to the patent language, then the easier it is for someone to find a chink in the patent's armor to manipulate the words in front of judge and jury to accomplish the desired litigious goal. Saul was of that sort of Pharisaical group. The Pharisees were legalists who deeply studied and partook in legalistic debate and enforcement regarding interpretation of the Torah. This is why Saul-Paul's wording is out of the ordinary. This is not specifically a bad thing, but it does allow for unjust loopholes to be found within his often confusing words that far exceed necessity.

The more wordy the legal text is, then the more abundant the opportunity for manipulation. Once a word is written, it then must be interpreted by the reader. When the ability to read is limited in a society, then the citizens of that society are at the mercy of those who can read. Thus they will be taught the meaning of the text through the eyes or interpretation of the person or people who can or want to read and preach to them. Sadly, in the modern era while most people can read, we simply do not, and thus we rely upon the priests' and preachers' interpretation of Saul-Paul's convoluted wording.

Authority of Discipline and Government of the Church

In past times long ago, not everyone could read like most people can in modern societies. In those days the Priests, Scribes, and Pharisees were the few who were educated and knew how to read. To best understand this, you have to first understand that books and paper or papyrus were quite rare and very expensive back then, so there was not an abundance of printed matter that people had in their homes—there were no **book**shelves. In fact they didn't even have the same need to read as we do today. Everywhere we look now we have text that we need to read, from road signs to menus to complex instructions. If there was anything that the general populous needed to read back in those days it would likely have been very brief. And if it was something such as a city direction sign most people are capable of recognizing a few words without needing to actually learn to read because that sign is then more of a whole symbol to them.

This lack of need to read placed the burden of teaching on the shoulders of the church leaders. There were no lengthy pharmaceutical labels to read or complex instructions to run a TV back then. The only text of substance that the citizens had and that they had any true interest in was the Torah. And since a document such as the Torah would have cost a great deal of money to painstakingly reproduce, no one in the general population could afford it anyway. Thus the task of teaching the Torah law was left to those who could read, such as the Priests, Scribes, and the Pharisees.

It is these who could read that were the authorities who established the societal rules of conduct that they derived from the Torah. These authorities would teach the Torah to the people and likely were asked tough questions by the people. These authorities would debate potential technicalities amongst themselves regarding the meaning of various statements made in the Torah and would record key aspects of their discussions regarding scrolls (scrolls are basically ancient books). You can think of these Talmud books much like a legal library. Saul-Paul was one such Pharisee authority.

Any large group needs some amount of guidance because inevitably our human nature will cause disagreement about something between any two people at some point. Authority that is just and true will mediate between the disagreeing parties. Back in the time around when Christ came, those authorities were the Priests, the Scribes, and the Pharisees and they used their Talmud-like interpretation of the Torah as their guide to resolve such disputes. But disciplined people who follow Truth have authority only when they follow Truth, which is where the problem entered regarding the tensions between The Christ and those authorities.

If Christ was in fact the very Word of God, then The Christ was the Ultimate Authority on Earth from that time onward. The people gravitated towards The Christ because He spoke with tremendous and True Authority. This was a massive challenge to the Priests, the Scribes, and to the Pharisees and they didn't like it, so much so to the point where they sought to kill Jesus The Christ which they eventually succeeded in doing.

But because Christ is the actual True Authority, He bestowed the earthly authority of his Church on to the eleven remaining Apostles. As the Apostles worked to increase the size of Christ's True Church, there were ever more people trying to share the message of the arrival of the Messiah and of His gift of Salvation. But like the "telephone game" where one person whispers something to the next person and so on, until it goes around a circle of people and returns to the original messenger somewhat changed to a point of complete disassociation to the original statement, so too did it occur with the news of The Christ and Salvation. Nowhere is this more evident than in the epistles of Saul-Paul. Saul-Paul's ability to conflate the message and cause people confusion made it easily possible for people to inadvertently or even deliberately manipulate his words to mean something that those words were likely never intended to imply, much like what dishonest lawyers and dishonest politicians do with the laws of the land in our modern era. This has always occurred throughout human history because we humans, for whatever reason, have an affinity to corrupt ourselves within Satan's world.

They didn't have the luxury of abundant print as we do today, so they had to explain it as best as they understood things and then hope the person they shared it with understood it correctly as they intended to convey it to them. A book such as the one you are reading now is able to be abundantly reproduced either on paper or electronically and will not change one bit between one person reading and then the next person reading it. But if you attempted to discuss it with others and then they share what you told them as they understood you and that continues for several iterations, you can be assured that the original intent of the statement would eventually and rather quickly get twisted into something that was not intended to be conveyed in the original text.

To best understand this, God told Isaiah, "Write down all these things I am going to do." God did not have Isaiah write it down for practice sake, it was to make a permanent record of the message so that Isaiah, or anyone thereafter, could examine that same text and interpret it firsthand. One problem that a holy book like the Quran has is that parts of it are *word-of-mouth* recollections of things Mohammed supposedly told those around him, and those statements were then gathered into one document sometime *after* Mohammed's death. So, some of the Quran is not as sound as other parts of it are because it may be third- or fourth-hand retelling of Mohammed's words. The Bible is different in that way because with the Bible those accounts were actually written deliberately to record them for accuracy while, or shortly after, the events occurred. However, there are a few books contained in the Catholic Bible that have been removed from many other Bible versions, books which the authority of is in question, so they are considered "Apocrypha" and some others are considered "Pseude-pigrapha"—More detail about these and other ancient writings can be found in the book *Understanding The Bible.*

Authority of Discipline, which is to say True Discipleship, was granted to Christ's eleven remaining Apostles, and over time as The Christ's Church grew, there came evermore disagreement until fundamental Church doctrine was eventually established and a sort of Church Government consisting of those who could read and teach became the church authorities.

Commit to Joy

This whole chapter is about commitment. The authorities committed themselves to relaying the messages of Salvation as accurately as they knew how. Commitment is a big deal to God. When we commit we are making a sort of covenant with the person or entity with whom we are committing. If you commit yourself to Truth and are also ever seeking Truth, then you will find Joy and be committed to it. Life is far less troublesome when we choose to commit to the path of Truth.

Committed Laws

Not all commitments are true or good. Many well-meaning people will make good and bad laws or write things that are not in accord with God where it became difficult to differentiate between the good and the bad law due to the tone and secondary meanings implied within them. Someone can say to you, "Oh, how I love you" and then punch you in the face mere moments later. This would likely confuse you because people who love someone do not intentionally or unjustly harm them. This is the typical result of laws and mandates that lack the fullness of Truth when handed down to the people of the society that those laws are intended to govern.

In the United States there's an implication of the "separation of church and state", but this is greatly misunderstood as is the True Church of Christ. In the United States of America the governing bodies are separated into distinct sections in effort to reduce the possibility for abuse of powers. A part of the United States' national document was to *not* have an established national religion. It was not intended to attempt to abolish religion altogether as some folks pretend to understand it. When all powers, including religion, are assembled into one body, it opens the door to dictatorships which is then followed by the people being controlled by a single person who may be good, but more often is entirely corrupt and selfish.

Of the making of laws there are many, but of people with an ability to reason in Truth there far too are few. For instance, there are concerns spread abroad by some "scientists" about the Earth's environment which many lawmakers wholly accept without question. These lawmakers then proceed to make laws in their futile attempts to address the concerns of these pseudo-scientists. But in so doing they seldom are able to solve any problems at all, and that's if said problem actually exists to begin with. Even the church gets in on this action with popes writing encyclicals on environmental concerns, etc. Not that this is wrong, but if the information that the church bases its information upon is not accurate, then the encyclical is invalid and yet remains within church doctrine and documents for the long-term, much the way that Saul-Paul's epistles still remain in church doctrine.

The problem with these laws is that they are seldom addressing the actual root of the problem, which church documents sometimes come closer to addressing, but often still generally miss the point. A polluting company can be ordered to clean things up by the courts that are enforcing the laws of the land, but the environmental problems are far more complex than just that, in fact they are so complex that they are at a personal level.

I can only assume that many readers will miss the point I am about to make, but Jesus told Peter to "feed my sheep." Now we all know that the "sheep" are the people, and that Peter was to feed them the Bread from Heaven, that is to say The Word of God. But in our modern era, while we do that, we tend to forget to teach them the process. Most people have likely have heard the saying, "Feed a man a fish and you feed him for a day, teach a man to fish and you feed him for life." But while that sounds good, it is only good for a single generation. I say to you to teach a man to teach men to fish and feed the world—*forever*!

And that is where these laws and some church encyclicals fall short. They seek to place a bandage on the problem rather than digging down deep to face the true problems head-on and then resolve the actual roots. If you get cut and place a bandage on your cut that is good, but if you fail to properly deal with that which cut you, then you will get cut again and again and again, and so will others who encounter the dangerous cutting edge. But if you teach others about the dangerous edge and why it is dangerous and then teach them to teach others about that same sharp edge and how to remove it, then the teaching can propagate for generations, thus giving each new generation the ability to reduce instances of sharp edges being exposed on which people would get cut. This eliminates others from being cut. But in this there is a problem which is that when a problem is well in control, the next generation might in fact be taught about sharp edges, but the teaching has less meaning to them because they have never experienced the trauma from a serious wound because the sharp edge was not there for them to get injured on. Their safety is due to the previous generations' diligence in the matter.

This is where the church and many parents have failed. We protect people and children to a point of inhibiting their ability to learn, and then we get lax on our teaching and end up causing the information to be altogether forgotten. When we teach a man to teach men to fish, we must also teach the lessons of *the failure to teach*. The Bible is one such teaching document that is mostly self-propagating, but even with that we fall short. The Bible is full of horror stories due to the failures of the people written about within it, all of which are invaluable lessons from which we can learn and then pass on to our children. But even the best of parents sometimes are unable to accomplish passing along such vital information. There are far too many preachers and teachers of the Bible whose children have strayed and never returned—This is a testament to our human failures.

If something sounds good and loving, it does not mean that it will achieve a good and loving outcome. Too many laws often end badly, and when the church jumps on this societal bandwagon we just might be entering a time of woe.

Hold On to Truth

During conversations I have had with various people that I encountered, it was found that many people inherently understand truth, but due to the noise of the world they have a difficult time finding it. A scientist says "the sky is falling" and far too many people say, "Run, the sky is falling!" instead of stopping and taking a rational look at the facts. I have spoken to people that have told me that there is no such thing as "truth" and that it is irrelevant and that only "facts" matter. It is almost impossible to respond to such an ignorant statement, but this is the way some people choose to see things.

Actual facts that are based in reality are true and we know that they are true through the process of Truth. Truth is base and it has a process and is a process. If a person is unable to tap into the process of Truth, then, as a technicality, they will be irrational in their thinking. Contemplate as to whether or not you use the process of Truth in your thinking. Do you consider things other people say, or do you immediately think "No, I don't accept that!" and then reject it immediately because it does not agree with what **you** want to hear or your current beliefs? Do you accept everything someone says just because you see them as some sort of authority figure on their particular subject of "expertise", or will you question things they say that seem out of order?

When you achieve Truth within you, do not let it go of it. Hold onto it even unto your very last breath. All good things arise out of Truth, and all bad things arise out of lack of Truth. Never deny Truth because doing so will cause you untold trouble and torment throughout your life and even eternally thereafter. Denying Truth in your early adult life can cause lasting painful ramifications that will follow you all of your days here on earth, even if you have since embraced Truth. This is not a punishment from God, but rather it is a result of our foolish actions. Defying Truth can permanently stain your pure white clothes as mentioned in an earlier section.

Offer Yourself

In the book *Red Hot Marriage* the correlation of the relationship between husband and wife, as compared to God and man, is discussed. The husband is in the God position and the wife represents the people. When a wife offers herself in fullness to her husband in an intimate manner, she physically and spiritually invites and allows him into her. We are to do similarly with God's Truth by opening up our hearts and allowing Truth to enter into us.

We are to offer ourselves by opening up and allowing Truth in and then embracing Truth and holding onto it to never let it go. This is the key component of being *at one* with God. When we do this, then the amount of sins we commit are greatly reduced. Not because we are given a pass on our foolish behavior, but rather because we will make fewer mistakes overall. While we are still somewhat imperfect and human and will potentially still make some mistakes, the Truth in us offers us a simple clarity that anyone can understand. It allows us to easily see and discern things that we should not say, do, or be involved in. What is best about Truth being in us is that the bad things or things that are bad for us no longer have the same level of irresistible appeal to us as they did before we embraced Truth.

If you ever wonder how an addict can suddenly just stop their addiction, then wonder no more. When the void within them that they filled with the addiction is instead finally filled with Truth, then the void no longer exists and no longer needs to be filled, and thus the person feels whole and the emptiness is then gone.

No one of man will ever feel whole without being at one with God; this is why *atone*ment in the Bible is such a big deal. You cannot be *at one* with God if Truth is not in you. We are made by God and are made and intended to be at one with God. We as humans can be uniquely individual, but without God we will always feel partly empty and will attempt to fill our emptiness with accolades from others. We do this by extreme behavior, such as bodily mutilation from piercings, tattoos, rallying to the latest trendy cause while being loudly vocal about it, or maybe by being aggressive in life so as to prosper so that people will like us or are impressed with our things or status. When you offer yourself and open yourself up and allow Truth to flow into you, then none of that is any longer of great importance to you and you will then feel peace and joy. When you are filled with Truth you may still have riches, but those riches no longer control you or your decisions. Instead, your decisions are based upon pure Truth, and your personal Peace and Joy are the result.

Chapter 11

Our Part

As we work towards Understanding The Church, we must visit some of these seemingly irrelevant topics—though they are not at all irrelevant. Our own little part of the True Church of Christ might in the big picture seem insignificant, but truly it is not. For you do not know today what impact your current actions will have tomorrow. Have you ever even thought to consider that something as simple as reading a book such as the one you are reading at this very moment can affect all of your tomorrows?

What if you have some striking thought that allowed you to invent something that was helpful and good for all of the world because some simple statement in this book provoked a thought in you that you would otherwise never have had? This means that you might have affected the entire world because you read words from the author of this book, and the author also might have been inspired by someone, resulting in a decision to write the book you are now reading. And on it goes all the way back to God's Creation of Adam and Eve.

Offer Gifts

Each and every one of mankind has been given gifts to share, and often we see those gifts in a big way in some people. Even though all people possess great gifts, it does not mean that all people will use their own great gifts. One thing that is certain is that God will have His way. While humanity might do evil time and again, humanity will always ultimately progress towards oneness with God. We are created to seek and create; this is inherent in us from being created in the image of God.

If we consider God as the singular point of reason and the ultimate curious entity, then we can get a better grasp on our own human desires when we understand that *we* are created in God's image. Is there anything God does not know? I have to answer both *no* and *yes* to that. God knows all that God created, but does not know what God has not yet created. "Ask, and it shall be given you; seek, and ye shall find; knock, and it shall be opened unto you". This had to be God's fulltime activity prior to the time of Creation.

Sometimes people, and sometimes even church leaders get the wrong impression and imagine that we are not supposed to question God or be curious about things. But there's a great difference between being curious, versus questioning God's obvious authority over all things. Sometimes people in their curiosity will challenge God's authority. Doing so never ends well for them, but when we use our curiosity to know God better, we then have this amazing tendency to improve the world and discover great things.

Those who empty themselves of the noise of this world and open themselves up to Truth will find that when Truth flows into them that then their mind will open up and **they will see**. With this new-found vision we can see the gifts within us because the fear of ridicule fades as the certainty of our gifts increases. Now the gifts which God endowed into you are not going to be negative or bad in any way, though they can be abused and used to diminish rather than to build up. And while your own personal gift or talent might conflict with the evil agenda of the world that we often see around us, if your gift is true, it will eventually become recognized for good when you use it wisely.

Your gifts are not for you to hoard. Jesus Christ gave us the parable of the talents, where talents were given to three people to care for while their master went away. Two of the people doubled their talents and one buried the only one he was given because he knew his master was a hard master and did not want to risk investing it. When their master returned he came to see what each man did with his talents and the first two explained to the master that they doubled the talents. Then the third man came forward with his one talent and told his master that he buried it because he did not want to risk losing it; thus his diligence in keeping his talent safe is good, right? Not so fast, the master called him a "wicked and lazy servant" and then took his talent and gave it to be cared for by one of the other two more diligent servants.

We typically think of this parable in terms of money and doing good things with that money and getting a return on it, but we all might want to revisit this and reconsider our current perspective. We are given talents, like you personally are talented at something and you are to offer your talent to man to further man towards God's purpose, and through it bring more joy to the world. Your talent could be the very thing you currently do for work. When your talent is used in accord with God's plan then your talent will flourish. If you fail to utilize your talent, you can expect that it will be stripped from you and others will do what you ought to have done with your talent. *They* will get credit for what *you* should have done with your talent. The credit for that talent was given to another because you refused to utilize it for the good of man. If you buried or hid your talent so that you would not lose it, or for fear of ridicule, then you are the "wicked and lazy servant".

Allow Truth into you and realize your good God-given talent and then use it for the betterment of your fellow man, and therein you will find joy and feel the fullness we all seek.

Ask and It Shall Be Given

This chapter is largely about the general concept of being open to receive. As mentioned in the last section, Jesus said "Ask, and it shall be given you; seek, and ye shall find; knock, and it shall be opened unto you." It is possible that many people fail to see the underlying point being made in that statement. It is about being open and curious. Not in some selfish manner, but open and curious to learn by using the process of Truth. God wants us all to seek answers to the questions we have about God and God's Creation. We are to explore space and the smaller realm of physics, but not to do so in spite of God, as is common in our modern era, but rather we must do so to discover God's Glory. We are also to discover our fellow man and even God directly!

If you accept the fact that there is a Creator God, then you must realize that the Creation events did not each happen in a "day" the way we sometimes want to interpret the events from the Creation account found in Genesis. Being that we are human and see things from our tangible physical earthly perspective, we tend to lose sight of God's perspective. The Creation topic is scrutinized in *The Science of God* books where *proper* interpretation of the Genesis Creation account is discussed. It was neither a big bang, nor did it occur in six twenty-four-hour days. God had unlimited time to Create the vast heavens and there is no way possible that any human will ever be able to exhaust the things to be discovered. In fact, collectively as the entirety of man we will never exhaust the hidden things to yet be discovered on just our home planet Earth alone.

We are Created to explore and wonder and learn and create, that is how we play as God's children. When we *ask*, *seek*, and *knock*, it shall be *given* and *found* and *opened* unto us. If you have not yet done so, pull your gifts out of the dark closet within you and dust your gifts off and polish them and place them somewhere they can be seen and enjoyed by those around you. Maybe it's something simple like making great food at the nearest restaurant or writing a new hymn. Use your talents well and they will multiply, and as they do, it just might so happen that you will find that the master will place you in charge of even more unrealized talents within you, thus allowing you to offer even more to your fellow man. And all you had to do is *ask* and then *receive!*

Accept Christ

As children, if we are taught about things in the Bible we are typically taught those things in an analogical manner. This happens because there are analogies in the Bible. Jesus' parables are analogies, and the parable of talents spoken of in this chapter is one such parable analogy. But we also inadvertently assume that many other things in the Bible are analogies and mere examples when most things in the Bible actually are not. If a person grew up in western culture in recent centuries, they were exposed to abundantly printed Bibles to a point where many statements from the Bible become little more than cliche to us. We see these Biblical statements as little witticisms because we hear them as the cliche statements many people use them as. It's a true tragedy that this occurs because it causes the real depth and meaning to become lost when doing so. We are always told by preachers to "Accept Christ", but often this profound term, turned cliche, is entirely missed by us.

Accepting Christ is more than just saying that you believe in Jesus. We can believe Jesus was a man who they hung on a Cross upon which He died. And we can then go further and accept that Jesus was The Word come into the world to save us as Promised by God to Adam and Eve. We can even go further and accept that this Word made Flesh who was Jesus The Christ not only died but astoundingly actually rose from the dead. And we can go yet further and accept that after Jesus rose from the dead He walked the earth for several weeks and that people spoke with him, and then we can further accept that he Ascended to Heaven. All of these things are events that we each must choose to accept, or to ignore.

With the act of "accepting" there are many levels and events and aspects that occurred which you can accept with regard to things of God. The items listed in the previous paragraph are a brief sampling of some of what we need to open our hearts and minds to. There is so much more there for us to accept, but be certain that this does not have the meaning that we should accept everything we hear when it sounds too good to be true. No, we must test these things before we receive them, even going as far as testing the statements by, or made about, The Christ in the Bible. Every generation must read and decide for themselves what they will choose to believe. But never forget that no matter what *you* choose to believe, your belief has no bearing on what is true and what actually happened and what things actually mean.

Receive the Word

You are a vessel made of dirt, for real! "And to dust you shall return" as it says in Genesis Chapter 3 in the Bible. You as a vessel will be filled with something—What will it be? Only you get to decide what you will be filled with. At birth we are filled with Truth and Light, but that quickly gets sucked out of us by the abundance of lies that we encounter coming at us from all directions in society from the very moment we are born.

Sometimes things are just given to us and we don't even have to ask for them. In fact, many of the things mentioned in the Bible are such things that we generally would not even have to ask for. But as our human nature would have it, we are our own personal fortresses that are so tightly closed that we become our own prisons. If you are closed, you will be incapable of receiving, and this can be true even if something is automatically given to you without you having to ask for it.

Imagine for a moment that you're digging in your yard and you hit something hard and find that it's a rock. Then as you dig the rock out so that you can plant your tree in that exact spot you grumble about the rock the whole time. When you finally get the dirty rock out, you then grumble as you take it and toss it over the embankment. Now, because you are closed, you never thought to do even the most insignificant examination of the rock which might have contained a gold nugget covered by the dirt. I give this example only to illustrate that something could sit before our very eyes and we won't even realize it and thus while it was given, even offered, it was not received by us. We receive the gift of air every moment we live and breathe, but sometimes things are more like the rock in the example just given here, where they pass by us without us ever noticing those gifts.

The Word of God is like air, you cannot escape it because it is everywhere. But as already mentioned, we are vessels of dirt and clay and we make ourselves fortresses that become our prisons. How does that happen? As babies we are born innocent and full of Light but with the blemish of "Original Sin". Then as we grow, that Light is all too often sucked out of us by society and by those around us. This happens through discouragement and ridicule, resulting in us eventually ending up shutting ourselves off from the world to become our own personal fortress-prison. This fortress-prison eventually becomes a vacuum within us causing us to become very selective of what we allow back in.

When we find things that give us even the slightest glimmer of feeling good, we then will crack open our gate just enough to let some new vice in. Things like drugs, alcohol, abusing the gifts of intimacy, and so on, are what we typically allow in us. We get the false feelings of satisfaction from these activities, but because they all only serve to suck ever more of the Light of Truth out of us, the vacuum becomes greater and greater with each encounter. As the vacuum-void becomes stronger, every time we crack the door open to get our fix of false love, our vices get pulled into that vacuum ever faster with more force in each successive encounter.

Accepting Christ is not enough and is not all that there is to it. Some people imply that if you accept Christ then it is inherent that all of the rest is part of that acceptance. While there is a correlation there, it falls short. If you reject Christ or Truth or the Word you then have rejected all of them and that is clear. But you can accept one without having accepted or rejecting the others; it's just that you were not aware that there is more to it than simply accepting Christ. If you only accepted Christ but did not receive Christ, then you do not possess Truth.

You can accept Christ, but fail to receive the Word, and in doing so you still not have opened the door of your fortress-prison beyond getting your fix of the vice of religion in this case. Christ is the Word made flesh; but the Word is also Truth. This is why people think that if you accept Christ then you automatically got the three-for-one deal. People eventually get to a point in life that they surrender and say that they accept Christ, and for a time they will feel very good about it because they got their fix of their religion vice as they attempted to fill some of the void within them. When you have been destitute and involved in illicit substances and activities and are finally brought to ruin, and then finally forfeit your will and accept Christ, the difference in the way you feel upon releasing all of that, and then accepting Christ, is substantial. It feels much better and offers you a euphoric feeling.

This is where it stops with far too many people who convert from their previous way of life when they accept Christ. We often quickly close our fortress door and coast on our euphoric feelings, sometimes for years until a similar vacuum is created within us all over again, and all because we were not told.

If you want to keep feeling euphoric the way you do when you accepted Christ, then you must open the windows to your fortress and let the air of the Word of Truth freely flow into you to fill that vacuum. Do it early on and learn Truth. Become familiar with Truth until you recognize it. If you are not able to recognize Truth due to your not allowing the Word of Truth into you, then it will be far more difficult for you to differentiate between lies and Truth.

Do not confuse this with knowing the difference between good and Evil. We can all see when someone does an evil action. Little children are especially sensitive to evil, but they become desensitized to evil over the years through constant exposure to societal pressures. While a lie is in fact evil, it is not necessarily going to be apparently so. Think about this for a moment: *a lie is* **specifically** *designed to deceive*. Someone could unintentionally give you incorrect information due to the perspective from which they witnessed something, but that is not a lie. A lie is very specifically intended to look like it is true with the explicit intent of deceiving the hearers of the lie. Sometimes when someone is inaccurate, what they are saying will not make sense and will sound almost irrational to us, thus allowing us to detect that something is amiss in their words. But if the detail they gave you is perceived as inconsequential when you hear it, then you might be none the wiser of their error in their words.

We sometimes "fib", which is likely derived from the word "fable". We often do this in order to misdirect people's attention so that we can do something special for them like a surprise birthday party or something on that order. While the "fib" is technically a lie, lies are usually far more consequential and almost always involve some sort of damage to property, person, or reputation, where some damage to the liar will occur if the lie is ever found out and truth revealed, which is something that is common in politics. Lies are designed to deceive. A well-built lie can deceive many of those who are unprepared. You cannot be prepared to cope with lies when you do not recognize Truth, and you cannot recognize Truth if you do not open the windows and doors to your fortress-prison to allow Truth to flow into you. It is when we allow Truth in *and* receive it that we begin to recognize Truth. A good start is to *ask* and it shall be *given*.

The book *Hot Water* discusses becoming accustomed to the water temperature in your shower and how when that temperature changes as someone else in the house uses the water in another room it causes you to quickly feel the water temperature change (typically more noticeable in older homes). Lies and deceit work the same way, and in a way so does Truth. If you live in an environment of lies, like our culture of modern "news" media offers, and you are never exposed to the truth of the matter, then you will not recognize that you are immersed in filthy boiling hot water. But when the cool clean refreshing water of Truth comes into the mix you will feel it, and often it will feel uncomfortably cold to you at first. But without the cool pure Truth you will eventually boil to death in the hot water of lies. Accept Christ and then open yourself up and received the Word of Truth along with Christ and live in Peace and Joy as God and Christ intend for you to live and be a part of the True Church of Christ.

Chapter 12

The Teacher is a Good Shepherd

There is a saying that goes "When the student is ready the teacher will appear". Not sure where that's from, but in regard to God it is entirely false and backwards. With God the teacher is always there patiently awaiting the student. Christ is the Good Shepard and we are instructed to follow Him. You probably have heard the phrase "follow the teachings of [so and so]". Teachers are shepherds, but not all of them are good. Far too many teachers are leading their flock of sheep to the edge of the cliff and many are leading the sheep over the edge, or in some cases they are deliberately pushing the sheep over the edge as they laugh at and mock them. Woe to those evil shepherds!

Any teacher who follows and then teaches Jesus The Christ's teachings and abides in them is a good shepherd. But as the church and its goodness ebbs and flows, the teachings can become unstable when they are reinterpreted by unscrupulous teachers and then indoctrinated into the unsuspecting sheep.

Revelations

The whole point of a teacher is to reveal **truths** to their students. The students can be in a school, or a college, or readers of a book, or even the congregation of a church where the teacher is the priest or preacher. All of them are meant to be revealing *true* things to the student-sheep that are there seeking answers and Truth. When people attend these venues they are not there to be taught inaccurate information—they want Truth and fact! But as life would have it, Truth and fact are becoming more and more rare with each passing day. With a little effort and a lot of hope we can probably reverse this evil trend, but we can also expect a bit of a battle in doing so. It's very sad to see, and it hurts even more to have to say that while there are many good shepherds in the church, there are also a few too many evil shepherds who have led their flocks to the edge of the cliff and are now in the process of casting each sheep over the cliff onto the rocky crag far below as they take joy in the destruction of each poor little sheep.

The Lamb of God

The Lamb
The Lamb of God
The Son Of Man
The Son Of God
The Word Made Flesh
The Word Of God
Redeemer
Savior
And Salvation
Our Lord
Lord of Hosts
King of Kings
The Way
The Truth

And The Life
Yeshua Ha Meshiach
The Messiah
Yeshua
Jesus The Christ
Amen, Amen, Amen
Amen
Amen, Amen, Amen

Some Things Are Apparent

When studying with an open heart and an open mind, we need not study long to understand that Jesus The Christ was in fact the arrival of the Promise made to Adam and Eve. Some things are quite apparent. Even the fact that a Creator must exist is made logically apparent by simply looking up in the night sky or the studying the workings of a tiny ant or a simple little flower pedal. Not everything is apparent, which is why we need **good** teachers. The teacher of Truth is ever present and is waiting for each one of us to open our door and let Truth flow into us.

It does appear that when we ask, then the teacher comes, but that is only an illusion. We must realize that we have to open our eyes enough to realize that we first have to ask. Once we realize that we have to ask, then we have to actually do the process of asking and then "the teacher will come". But the teacher only appears to come; it's just that you didn't recognize that the teacher was standing right before you the whole time eagerly waiting to answer your questions as you are able to receive those answers.

Sometimes things can get confusing for people, like for instance in knowing who The Good Shepard is. But who even catches these petty details in the first place? Jesus indeed was the Sacrificial Lamb who died for the vindication of Original Sin. That human Lamb of God who was the son of man being far superior to typical humans is well suited to guide us to the Spirit of Truth.

The Ten Commandments

A part of the teaching of the Good Shepherd that is made clear for those who are seeking and asking and knocking, is that the "Law" was being misinterpreted and misapplied by the Priests, Scribes, and Pharisees. This is a tricky subject to discuss when not fully elaborating on it, but the Mosaic "Law" is typically considered to be a bunch of guidelines laid out in the Torah, or those first five books of the Bible. Some of the guidelines were very important to abide by and others of them were more of a notification of danger and a remedy for problems, many of which were in regard to good health habits. But the legalist Pharisees opined on these guidelines, and through years and years of accumulated opinion, they began to make their collective opinion the "Law", rather than respecting the guidelines as stated in the Torah. And at times they utterly ignored the actual law of the Ten Commandments, for instance, by violating "Thou shalt not kill" as they sought to put Jesus to death, or "Thou shalt not bear false witness against thy neighbor" as they lied to deceive people about Jesus.

Jesus spoke lowly of the "law" in regard to the way that the Pharisees interpreted the law. And Jesus summarized the Ten Commandments down to only two when he said: "And thou shalt love the Lord thy God with all thy heart, and with all thy soul, and with all thy mind, and with all thy strength: this is the first commandment. The second is this: Love your neighbor as yourself. There is no commandment greater than these."

Because of the misinterpretation of parts of some of the epistles, many people have strayed from following the Bible. Take for instance the guidelines in the Old Testament stating that we should not eat swine flesh. Is it a sin to eat swine flesh? Not exactly; while we are told to not do so, we are not punished unto death or sent to hell for consuming it. Rather, we are found to be unclean and are supposed to take certain actions for a brief period and then we become clean again. There are many things like this in the Old Testament that are considered to be a part of the "law", but these points were abused by the opining Priests, Scribes, and Pharisees as they sought to impose their own interpretation of these guideline "laws" onto the people. You will catch this in Christ's dialog if you are watching for it–Because remember, "Seek and ye shall find".

Because of the way the epistles are interpreted, many people believe that the prohibition on swine flesh was invalidated because of a dream Peter had and things that Saul-Paul said. The point of Peter's dream was not that it was good to eat swine flesh, but rather that it is not going to damn you to hell, and if you are in a situation of teaching people and need to consume some "unclean" meat in the form of swine flesh, it will not damn your immortal soul to hell, rather you're just unclean for a while. And further, those who were not of Israelite descent were not to be shunned because they were not "clean", they too are worthy to be saved through the Promise fulfilled through The Christ. So this misinterpretation of a dream has come to a point where the church will often have pork luncheons. While this will not damn your mortal soul, it does fly in the face of God's instructions in the first five books of the Bible. What we have to ask ourselves about the Old Testament guidelines are things like this: What was the purpose for the prohibition of swine flesh? I will leave that for you to ponder.

Because we have been taught to believe in a fairy-god who magically and arbitrarily does and says things, we miss the fact that the actual real God does and says **all** things **for specific cause**. There is a reason behind each and every instruction in the Bible, eventually each will become apparent to you, but not without your asking. Remember, "Ask, and it shall be given you; seek, and ye shall find; knock, and it shall be opened unto you." Jesus wasn't trying to create some new trendy cliche with that statement–He meant it! And when you apply it to the Old Testament, things get really interesting.

Jesus wanted people to follow those guidelines as well as the actual Commandments, of which there are Ten. What Jesus sought to overcome in his dialog was the leaven of the Pharisees where they added their own and their predecessors' opinions to those guidelines and then claimed their leavened opinion to be "law", which they then unjustly imposed upon the people.

Accept and Obey Papal Authority

In the Catholic church you are told to obey the direction of the Pope. This sounds logical since the popes are understood to be the successors of Simon-Peter the Apostle of Jesus The Christ who Christ told he would establish his Church upon. We would expect that the church would then be teaching Christ's ways above all else. But it is actually the catechism of the Catholic church that governs church doctrine and is being taught to Catholics young and old alike. All Catholics are supposed to read the catechism and follow it and above all obey the Pope regarding authority and church discipline. If you fail to do so or violate this you are in a sort of schism with the Catholic church. This does not carry the same weight in society as it once did, because now society of a very secular nature dominates the world and even dominates the church, which is largely the fault of the Catechism itself.

Laws of the Church

Canon law of the Catholic church is a reasonably stable set of rules of the church stating regulations for the church regarding certain do's and don'ts defining terms much like typical modern law does, although it is a great deal shorter than modern laws. But this should give you an idea of the church law.

While the authority of the popes, otherwise known as Papal Authority, is in theory passed on down from Simon-Peter, we have to be cautious of our interpretation regarding this authority. This is one place where knowing Truth and allowing it to flourish within you is important. If a Pope goes wayward, as they sometimes do, we must reject their error and risk schism. For it is better to resist a rogue Pope than to spend eternity in hell.

In our modern era, it is becoming increasingly important to get printed copies of older Bibles and church doctrine because in the modern digital era when these documents are published publicly in textual digital form, the document can be easily altered from one day to the next day when you might view it. And with the Bible, unless you have read it many times over, you would be none the wiser about any changes that might have been made to the text. Digital technologies are really a great tool, but with all things abuses do occur. So if at some point, those in power decide that they don't like the way something is stated, they then can make a change of a few words to alter the entire meaning of a sentence or of an entire paragraph. Because the change seems minor, no one will notice—if they ever even read it at all. Then a bit of time elapses and a new group of people are born and taught from the edited version not even realizing any change ever occurred. Now, if the changes to the text are made in honesty in effort to adhere to Truth then it is all well and good, but if not, then the readers of the text will be deceived. This cannot happen when you own older printed versions of these documents.

I urge everyone, whether or not you care about such things, to get your hands on older copies of Bibles. I say older copies of Bibles due to the ease and abundance of printing in the modern era where there are many versions of the Bible, parts of which are not well translated; much more care was put into translating the early-Reformation era Bibles than is found with some Bibles today. Digital photographic image file copies of these are easy to acquire and are typically available for free or at relatively low cost, and because they are photographic images of old Bibles, they are unlikely to have been altered. If you are ambitious you can print your digital copies out at your leisure. Get your Bibles now while you still can, several in fact, and have them in your home, because if any digital text or newly printed Bible text is changed you then will always have your authoritative printed copies to fall back on. *Understanding The Bible* discusses which versions can be considered authoritative and why. Consider this paragraph an alert that you will not want to ignore.

Obey the Government!

Similar to opening yourself up to Truth and being able to defy the Pope if the need arises due to corruption and evil, the same is true of the government. It is becoming increasingly apparent that some countries have government leadership that is getting out of control with their authoritarian dictates that they have been forcing onto their citizens.

The "Obey the government" ideology is wrong. This is adopted from a statement of error in one of the Pauline epistles in the Bible written to the Romans. We must obey Truth and nothing other than Truth. If you obey any government official or any of the church hierarchy, even the Pope, and they are instructing you into error, then you are denying Truth and putting in its place man's rules. This was the very thing that Christ was sent to defeat. Eve listened to Satan rather than Truth. While we could be making an innocent error at times, wrong teaching is often not innocently done by the "shepherds". It is of no matter who is teaching the error. If you follow that teaching and abide by its errors your soul is in severe danger because you are then denying Truth.

Christ's messages are clear on this when we take the time to articulately read through the Gospels with all of our prejudicial Pauline biases dropped. Christ told us, in advance, that we would be persecuted for His sake. So you can expect that of the bodies of power who attempt to enforce man's laws onto you, laws that are not in accord with Truth, will not like you defying the government, or the church for that matter. And you can, and likely will, experience trouble by standing for Truth.

Blind Guides, the Church Authorities

The book *The Science of God Vol 1* reveals the reality of Creation in a way that is logical by explaining how Creation is really quite scientific and very deliberate, and it is not accidental or from some spontaneous event. When we begin to grasp the reality of Creation and how the Creator separated the waters above from the waters below (Spoiler alert, that part of Genesis is not speaking about the clouds and seas), it changes our perspective of just how real "Heaven" actually is.

I find that the perverting of the Genesis text was the key that evil used in order to bring down the church, and it has worked spectacularly well for evil, but not so well for the church. The church once championed science, and then when real true discovery occurred it was suppressed by the Catholic church. The church still champions "science" but no longer finances it like it did during the Renaissance era.

Today, instead of leading in science, the church leaders simply choose to believe what they are told about science and then gravitate towards that belief. Often we can feel this in sermons of individual priests, or maybe even in the encyclical writings of the popes. When this occurs in churches and in schools, as long as it is true we're okay, but when the information is not correct then we have a problem—a very big problem.

The blind guides in a church that teach error in that way are what Christ meant when He talked about the "blind leading the blind". When these things happen, it is good to know Truth and to know Truth well. One way to test this is when you legitimately suspect that you are being taught error and you properly and politely attempt to ask questions but are then beat down for an innocent question, then you can be pretty sure there are lies in your midst. People who speak Truth might get irritated by defiant people who speak foolish antagonistic things against Truth, but they will seldom get angry when legitimately challenged. If you truly know and embrace Truth you will invite scrutiny to test your thoughts, but when people are lying, they do not want scrutiny. In John chapter 3, Jesus commented about how "people loved darkness instead of light because their deeds were evil." Liars do not want scrutiny because scrutiny is light, and light brings forth Truth, and lies cannot stand in the face of Truth. Liars will suppress information and belligerently demand their lying voice be heard and the voices of Truth be suppressed.

Moon Worship

If you seek every verse in the Bible that mentions the moon, and read those verses in context, you might be surprised at what you find that those verses actually say. Some of the things said regarding the moon may very well have translator favorable predisposition influence written into them. In general, God was not pleased with certain things regarding the moon and people's affinity for those things. As alluded to in an earlier part of this book, it is a great error to base Christ's death and Resurrection on the phases of the moon. This causes the recognition and celebration of the Resurrection of our Savior to be inconsistent from year to year, sometimes bouncing around like a Ping-Pong ball from year to year, and worse yet, it separates the celebration of the Resurrection weeks apart depending upon where you live on Earth. This is moon worship in that we then are allowing the moon to dictate when the memorial celebration of Christ's Crucifixion, Death, and Resurrected are to be honored within any calendar year.

Aligning holidays with the moon is not bringing harmony to Christ's Church. It only serves to divide us. Sure we have survived for centuries under this error, but doing something wrong for many centuries does not make it right. We have been instructed how to calculate time using the celestial bodies, but for some reason even with the ancient writing still available to us we somehow cannot seem to get the church's calendar right. This all goes back to Passover and how that was calculated as to the particular time of year. Very simple, clear, and concise instructions were given in the Old Testament in this regard. If you become aware of this and look for it, that it to say "Ask and it will be given to you; seek and you will find; knock and the door will be opened to you. For everyone who asks receives; the one who seeks finds; and to the one who knocks, the door will be opened" then you will find it. Even when you carefully read the Gospels you will begin to detect some perception discrepancy if you do so with all of that in mind. Seek Truth and Truth will be revealed to you.

Bring Forth a Church

When we "Ask and it will be given to you; seek and you will find; knock and the door will be opened to you. For everyone who asks receives; the one who seeks finds; and to the one who knocks, the door will be opened" as Jesus said to us, then things begin to become apparent to us. But the lies of the world suppress that in us by inferring that we are not allowed to ask questions as can be read in the Catechism towards the beginning where it says "...let them in the humility of faith, believe and adore all the mysteries contained in this Article, and not indulge in a curious inquisitiveness by investigating and scrutinizing them—an attempt scarcely ever unattended with danger."

When we ask questions, we often are challenging someone's authority. Have you ever questioned a doctor? Some of them do not like *you* asking *them* questions that challenge their words. You will notice this with some priests and preachers and many school teachers as well, especially with college professors. If you ponder this authoritarian attitude situation, you will likely find one of three things: First it is possible that someone is simply having a bad day and was easily agitated and they lashed out for no good reason. The second possibility is that the person doesn't have answers and is only repeating what they were taught and is becoming frustrated because they are unable to answer your questions properly. And finally, the person is possibly a liar or believes lies and your questions are beginning to expose those lies. Sadly it is the latter of these three that is the more common circumstance when such conflict occurs.

When you open yourself up to Truth and embrace Truth, you will begin to learn Truth's methods, thus allowing you to answer many questions with deeper understanding. I will assume that most people understand what is being conveyed in the previous paragraph. Now imagine a world with no TVs, or electronic devices with which to look things up to research them on your own. Imagine this world with books and scrolls being a treasured rarity that only the most "educated" had access to or could afford. Now with the previous paragraph in mind imagine asking one of those who had access to these scrolls a question or challenging that authoritarian's words. The information differential during that historical era was much greater than it is in the modern era. There are books everywhere in modern times, so we have the ability to self-educate. This was *not* the same situation thousands of years ago.

In Christ's day the people had to rely on the Priests, Scribes, and Pharisees to give them information. This is why Christ so very quickly gained a following. He spoke the Truth and did not berate people or silence them for asking questions. He actually did the opposite and told them things even before they had the chance to ask him. What he told them was helpful for them and they drew to his Truth like a magnet to steel.

If you pay any attention to the world of broadcast entertainment and the "news", you should have a good indication as to why the Pharisees were out to defame and crush The Christ. He was taking their audience by doing nothing more than giving them Truth. The lies of the Priests, Scribes, and Pharisees could not stand against Christ's Truth, so they had him killed. Sound familiar at all? This is common behavior with liars; they defame and destroy to attempt to conquer the territory that they want to protect and to hide their lies. But they have no choice if they choose to continue in their lies, because only a little match can light a whole room and expose their lies lurking within.

We end up having this sense that Peter started the Church, but it was Christ who established the Church and He brought forth the Church through Truth. He then placed that infant Church into the arms of Simon-Peter so that when endowed with Truth it could be carried through the ages. Despite the many errors of Catholic church leaders over the years, Christ's Church thrives all around us. But just as Christ was a gentle soul showing kindness, love, and compassion while standing firm and uncompromised in Truth, so too does his *True* Church.

Chapter 13

Fluidity of a Changing Church

There is no question that the Catholic church has had its ups and downs over the centuries. Different popes and leaders come into leadership positions with their own understanding of things and they work to insert that understanding into the church doctrine. Their understanding could be in error, but it will be entered in to the doctrine nonetheless. Some of these ideas cause division within the church to a very troubling end. But often they change the church either in good or in bad ways without actually dividing the church. The church changes much the way government does, but typically at a far slower pace, which is good. The church deals in souls, the governments deals in money and things.

We do not want a church making kneejerk decisions like the governments do just because some group was whining that they didn't like what a priest said. Unfortunately, this has been increasingly occurring in many churches around the world at an ever more rapid pace, and it must stop now. It seems that the only people that the church has been ignoring are those who want to return to Truth. Yes, the Catholic church does change and it is not always good, sometimes the changes are very bad and drive away the people of the True Church as happened in the early part of the twenty-first century. In the governments of many countries, we have the ability to vote bad leaders out so long as they are not cheating in the counting of the ballots. But within the Catholic church it's more of a dictatorship with little dictators randomly placed within the hierarchy, yet this too shall pass. The church will soon become desolate at its current pace. Getting angry at this fact does little to remedy the problem of this dying patient.

Man's Rules

Because the church has so long depended upon the words of Saul-Paul in its teaching, the church is unable to rid itself of the Pharisaical DNA inserted by Saul-Paul. The DNA being referred to is that of *authoritarianism*, and whether deliberate or innocently-habitual it is there due to Saul-Paul's Pharisaical habits as well as from human nature.

There is little more that we need to know about Christ than what Christ and the Prophets said. There is a very important distinction that people need to make in regard to the books of the Bible which is further explained in the book *Understanding The Bible*, where it explains why various sections and books of the Bible carry different weight in their level of authority and significance in regard to your Salvation. The items with the least authority are Saul-Paul's epistles. You might wonder why someone would speak such "blasphemy" against Saul-Paul. Paul may have crossed paths with Christ, but he never really met or knew him.

I don't recall any mention of it, but it is very possible that Saul-Paul was witness to Christ's crucifixion and possibly may have been party to it, though because he is "Paul of *Tarsis*" and not being from the specific area where Christ was Crucified, the chance is low. Regardless, he did not know Christ personally and would not have been a follower of Christ at any point before Christ's Resurrection and Ascension.

Saul-Paul was nothing more than a preacher just as we have today. This does not take away from any good things that he may have said or any good that he may have done. But let's keep things in perspective here; Saul-Paul was a Pharisee and he talked and behaved like a Pharisee as can be witnessed in his letters. His influence has affected people and even brought people to Christ, but it has also caused many to veer down wrong paths due to their own misinterpretation of his convoluted words. I realize that I am being a bit harsh in discussing Saul-Paul, but pay attention to the level of attention his misinterpreted words often get over The actual Christ's clear and concise words. Most "Christian" churches have built their doctrine upon Saul-Paul's words. This doctrine in turn becomes the rules and teaching for the congregation, it is man's rules, rather than God's or Christ's rules.

The Infallible Teacher Pope

With man being the humans that we are and, unfortunately, quite easy to corrupt, for us to speak of any human beyond Christ as "infallible" is simply foolish. Assuming that when Jesus conferred onto Simon the Title "Peter" (Petra, Pater, Father) that Peter would speak to perfection is error on our part. Not that Peter was wrong, but that his ability to think about something incorrectly still existed in his human nature. This is made evident by his dream about making all things clean where he said "Absolutely not, Lord, for I have never eaten anything that is common or unclean!" In reply, a voice told him, "Get up, Peter! Kill something and eat it." This simple vision illustrates that even Simon-Peter, the rock of Christ's Church, could harbor thoughts that are not in full accord with God's will.

The idea in the Catholic church is that Peter's title and authority should be passed down from one papal foundation to the next. The Catholic church believes that this is done through the popes. Papal authority reigns supreme in the Catholic church and will usurp the will of God when a pope sees fit. Now, we can assume that many people will take the position that since Peter's authority was conferred onto each successive pope that they then become infallible. But as history shows all too well, this is simply not the case. Consider for example the "Indulgences" debacle of the Reformation era.

Making any human out to be infallible is a foolish mistake and diminishes the need for Christ to have ever even come to save us from the Original Sin of Adam and Eve. If we were perfect, then maybe we too could have broken the bonds of Satan's power for each our own self. While some popes may make themselves out to be God, "gods" the popes are not! Some popes might be spiritually more pure than most people are, but infallible they are not. Should we listen to any pope to hear what they have to say? Probably, but with judicial reserve. This goes back to allowing Truth to flow into you and getting to know Truth and Truth's process of discernment. What does Jesus Say about this? "But Jesus, aware of their malice, said, 'Why put me to the test, you hypocrites? Show me the coin for the tax.' And they brought him a denarius. And Jesus said to them, 'Whose likeness and inscription is this?' They said, 'Caesar's.' Then he said to them, 'Therefore render to Caesar the things that are Caesar's, and to God the things that are God's.'"

Render unto the Pope the things that are the Pope's and unto God the things that are God's. Yes, Christ's Church has great authority on Earth, but as a whole rather than as a single individual. Should we even have a pope sitting in the seat of Peter? Possibly. What is done in other non-Catholic churches has not proven to work any better as a form of church governance, so it is probably indifferent. If we back up all the way back to the Israelites' Exodus from Egypt and shortly after they entered their "Promised Land", they wanted a king, but God wanted them to self-govern because as was historically proven time and time again, earthly kings have a tendency to oppress the people whom that king serves. Christ himself said that we must serve others, and he even went so far as to wash the filthy feet of his Apostles as an example to show such service.

God's Rules

When kings or peasants come into a position of power, in Christ's eyes that person is supposed to be the servant of those whom they are there for. I cannot imagine that this would be any different just because we decided to call someone a "pope". In our world filled with mankind, we make rules, and lots of them. Many of these rules are oppressive; however, basic fundamental rules typically are not oppressive as they serve a utilitarian purpose for the people. When our rules become convoluted or perverted, they always serve specific people, with prejudice against all others.

This occurred world round in the early part of the twenty-first century when good shepherds spoke against the evil that was being perpetrated through the Catholic and other churches. These good shepherds where silenced and removed from the parishes that they so successfully shepherded. These good shepherd-priests gained much attention and their church attendances surged because people wanted to hear Truth being preached. Yet, the Pope did nothing to stop corrupt bishops and cardinals from silencing Truth as they removed these good shepherds from those churches.

When these good-shepherd-priest-servants of God spoke of God's rules they were silenced and cast out by the "authorities" of the Catholic church. If this confuses you or places you in any mental contradiction with regard to "papal authority" then you likely do not embody Truth. Pour out such prejudices and allow Truth to flow into you, and then God's rules will become apparent to you, thus allowing you to follow the will of God, rather than the will of man.

A Congregation of Many

Christ's Church has remained constant over the past couple of millennia, but the Catholic church has not. The Catholic church hierarchy has been relatively stable when viewing it from the outside, but in truth it is greatly fragmented when looking deeper into the situation. Most people don't ever ponder where all of the various Christian religions are from. We generally don't question these things; we just sort of subconsciously assume they all spontaneously sprung up and that they are all relatively good. But there is a connection to all of these religions that is both apparent and not so apparent. Obviously these so-called "Christian" religions all claim that Jesus was The Christ, but there is a simpler and more recent connection.

After Christ's Ascension, the Apostles and those they taught went abroad and spread the Good News that the Promised Savior has come and Salvation was at hand. After word-of-mouth sharing of this long-awaited news, the messages began to get a bit corrupted through that very same word-of-mouth sharing as mentioned earlier in this book, remember the "Telephone Game"? To reduce these problems, the people convened to codify the doctrine in a creed. It is good because those who were close to the center of all of this could come together and all share the version they each had of their account of Christ and then together with the various books of the Bible and the writings of the Apostles, the council was able to construct a full picture of the story of Salvation using the details that were in full agreement, and then cast out or set aside things inconsistent with those details and that were also inconsistent with the books of the Bible's Old Testament and other ancient writings concerning the topic.

This convening of people became formalized as a universal assembly. The congregation of people is the "ecclesia" otherwise known as the "Church". We use words like *church, ecclesia,* and *congregation* more carelessly with each passing year, thus causing such words to lose their intended meaning.

Let us take for instance the word "Catholic", what exactly does it mean? Translated words are often translated phonetically when the word is used as a label or name or if there is no specific word to compare it to in the new language into which it is being translated. "Catholic" is one such word. The Greek term "katholikos" has two parts *kata* or *kath* meaning *in accord with* or *agree*, and *holos* meaning *whole*. Together they mean *the whole in agreement*. Thus, no matter where you were to go in the entire world, there is a universal message of Salvation which all members agree on regarding its content, thus "Catholic" has an underlying ultimate meaning of *universal salvation message*.

This "universal" church was open to all who would receive this message, and for over a thousand years things progressed well and the *whole assembly*, implied in the Greek name *katholikos*, remained for the most part, whole. But during the time preceding the Reformation era, devout Catholic Martin Luther began to question some of the newly imposed papal dictates regarding "indulgences". There also had been troubles brewing in other areas besides with Martin Luther. But at that time **everyone** was considered to be "Catholic" (katholikos). And to be honest about this, religion in the way we think of it in the modern era did not exist then. You believed the universal message, or you were a Jew of one of three sects (Pharisee, Sadducee, or Essene), or you were a non-believer. And the only difference between Catholics and Jews was the question of Jesus The Christ being the Promised Savoir. There weren't divisions at every turn during the devout Catholic Martin Luther's time. When Martin nailed his ninety-five theses to the door of the Castle church in Wittenberg, Germany it was a spark that set off an unquenchable fire.

With all of the mini-skirmishes within the Catholic church getting ever more heated, the kindling was ready for combustion. The fallout took a bit of time, but when the church pushed back against the looming Reformation it caused a rebellion against papal authority and ultimately division within the church. At some point those who agreed with Martin Luther were labeled as "Lutherans", even though Luther at the time did not want to divide the congregation in the way that eventually occurred. In addition to this, King Henry the VIII of England was having marital issues regarding children and wanted to have his marriage annulled, but the pope would not acquiesce to the King's unreasonable demands. This caused the King to declare a national religion now referred to as the "Church of England" or the "Anglican church". It is important to note here again that the term "church" means *ecclesia* or *congregation* or "to call the people". At this point the Catholic church was now broke up into three distinct major sects. Oh, and it didn't stop there.

While those who remained with the official Catholic church did stay together as a fairly stable group, the newly deemed Lutherans and the Anglican church did not. The Anglican church has less fragmentation, but the sects that arose from the Lutheran sect are numerous.

In truth these three main sects could still really all be considered as "universal" because if you were to go to an Anglican mass or a Lutheran mass or a Catholic mass you will not see a great deal of differences. The Anglican Church of England broke off from the papal authority only for the sake of the King's personal political agenda. Where the Lutheran side of the schism is a bit more nuanced, yet still largely in accord with basic Catholic beliefs.

A "church" is the *ecclesia* or the *congregation* which consists of *the people* and it is many. I feel safe in saying that if people truly understood the True Church of Christ that the existing church buildings could not contain all of the people who would eventually come. A "Church" is a congregation of many people.

Chapter 14

The Church is Alive

Our world can be a confusing place, especially with regard to politics and religion. In the political realm we often hear the term "progressives". Some people see this as a positive while others see it as very destructive. Some of this is borne out of the Catholic church's refusal to accept newfound truths in past times, like when they sought to suppress Galileo's findings about the Earth's place relative to the Sun. This sort of suppression of Truth harms everyone involved. The problem in politics is that the progressive movement does the exact same thing in an opposite manner. Just for the sake of rebelling against authority while pretending it is "progress", progressives will try to silence those who oppose their goals, and to do so they will suppress Truth at any cost. And then they further go on to claim the likes of Galileo as one of their own.

It does not matter who is suppressing Truth, whether it is the church of progressives, the renaissance era Catholic church, the church of science, or any other group—it is evil to do so. The Christ's True Church is an unchanging Church and it is alive and is in fact a Universal Church that always progresses toward knowing God better.

An Active Church

If you wonder how you can test a church to see if it is in accord with Christ's teaching you have two fallback methods: The first is to compare the doctrine and, even more importantly, compare the actions of a church to the words spoken by Jesus The Christ that are written in the Gospels for your convenience. Then as a secondary test, you can examine what a church is teaching; does it champion Truth along with good and Godly human achievement, or does it suppress it?

A truly active church that is seeking God and Truth will be on a consistently ongoing human achievement quest that includes God and Christ at every turn. It will not suppress Truth or promote lies. It will teach Truth and about Christ and of God's Promises fulfilled with its every move. It will not stop or suppress any exploration that is working to know God and God's Creation better.

But if a church fails to progress, then God will allow those who are not of Christ's church to achieve what had rightfully belonged to Christ's Church so that mankind can inch closer to God. We are to "Ask and it will be given to you; seek and you will find; knock and the door will be opened to you. For everyone who asks receives; the one who seeks finds; and to the one who knocks, the door will be opened."

If you ever heard the term "You snooze, you lose" well, it applies to The Christ's True Church. We are supposed to be an active Church, ever learning and ever teaching God's Glory through our work and through our every word. Be active and progress with Truth, or choose progress without Truth and perish and thus, allow the heathen to do and get credit for the work you were assigned but failed to do. Be active in Truth always!

Life of a Congregation

The life of a congregation can be measured in various ways. Often church buildings are constructed by a single generation, and to that generation and their children, their church temple is a treasure. As that generation dies off and their children and grandchildren take over, the passion slowly dissipates with subsequent generation and eventually the whole of the congregation dies from an exodus of the congregation. When attendance reaches a low enough level, the church-patient is pronounced dead and the church building closes because it is now only an empty building.

There was a time when it was somewhat opposite and the buildings were abandoned because they were not able to contain the growing congregation, so they built a larger church temple nearby. Not so in recent times. The churches are now emptying at an alarming rate, much like watching a stock chart graph on the downside of a stock boom. People will fool themselves by telling themselves that things are going good every time the graph ticks up a bit where the graph will go up one, but then it goes down two. The up-one-down-two sequence has been occurring for many decades in the universal churches. The entire Catholic church is in dire trouble, including the Lutheran and Anglican sects of the church along with their derivative religious sub-sects.

The life of a congregation will be robust and will last, but only as long as the fullness of Truth is shared with that congregation and the congregation remains a family. But beware, the moment lies are fed to the congregation you can consider that congregation soon to be dead. For a church cannot live without Truth. Truth was, and is, the whole point to begin with, thus there is no point without it. The Word of Truth coming for our Salvation was the Promise made to Adam and Eve and is what generations of people sought and are still seeking. We are the recipients of years of effort and waiting done by those before us, and we are able to see the history of those who waited, from whom we can learn the good things that they left for us, or perish by following their errors.

Building the Next Congregation

Can the dead come back to life? Jesus The Christ appears to have illustrated that it is not only possible, but He actually made it occur. The real question is: Can a dead *church* come back to life? Do we scrap the existing Catholic church, or do we tear the temple down and rebuild it?

This is all going to depend upon if that church has any bit of a discernable pulse left in it. Is it dead on arrival? Only time will tell. With the abominations inhabiting the Catholic and other church temples early in the twenty-first century, it is not looking very hopeful. Have we been alerting the rest of congregation about the errors of the church? Are we even trying?

When such abominations enter the church and are not removed, it causes desolation of the church. And at the rapidly increasing pace of such abominations being set up in the church temples, the church will be dead in little more than a decade. The church of the early twenty-first century was in severe peril with many truly good shepherds being silenced by internal corruption, all while corrupted clergy-wolves in sheep's clothing were allowed to continue ravaging the flocks. The church's burial will need to be prepared if we continue to allow these wolves to become too numerous and stay in power. Do we let the church die of its own accord, or do we try to save the world's Catholic church from itself?

Novus Ordo

Novus Ordo Missae, or the "New Order of Mass", was promoted by Pope Paul VI in 1969 as the result of Vatican II.

Back in the second half of the twentieth-century when Vatican II was established, the goal was, in concept, to make the mass more familiar and more understandable to the people. So the long-standing tradition of Latin mass was eventually removed from most churches and replaced with a shorter mass done in each area populations' native tongue using the Novus Ordo liturgy. There was also the issue of which direction the priest would face while doing mass, which had previously been *ad orientem* (toward the East). So the result of Novus Ordo was for the priest to turn towards the congregation during their native tongue liturgy.

Many churches of the early twentieth century had elaborate alters with a wall of ornate structures before it, often containing statues set inside of little alcoves. This would be set up behind where the priest now stands in a typical Novus Ordo mass when the priest is facing the congregation. But when those ornate altars were still in the churches, the priest would face the elaborate structure, typically facing east while saying mass in Latin with his back to the congregation.

Many people were upset with the implementation of Vatican II's liberal Novus Ordo approach and the church's new alter set-up and the new mass. Change is sometimes a slippery slope that is all too steep. If we could make things more understandable *and* more relatable and leave it at that, then we would have the winning formula. If only! But alas, that is not the case. Change can be a good thing when properly managed, but change has within it the DNA of *change*, and change breeds change. Whether good or bad will come of change, can only ever be known through time and testing. But know this; when change occurs and something doesn't seem quite right, we then have to quickly question if that change was good, or if we have gone too far.

While the intentions of Vatican II and Novus Ordo were likely mostly pure, it has not gone as may have been planned. It's difficult to tell for certain if Vatican II and Novus Ordo were the sole cause of the great exodus from the church or if societal pressures of that time were also the driving force, but in either case the timing fits perfectly. Many who want to return to the ancient Latin Liturgy believe that Novus Ordo caused the downfall of society. We can easily assume that it was a combination of such factors as were just mention that precipitated the great Catholic exodus of the twentieth and twenty-first centuries, but regarding the downfall of society at large, that is a different story.

Once the problem began it was like a boulder rolling down a mountainside gaining force and speed with each turn of the boulder. And then with each passing year the mountain seems to get bigger and higher to allow the boulder to roll ever faster until it began crashing early in the twenty-first century.

Whether Vatican II and Novus Ordo were at all to blame, we may never really know for sure because it was around that same time that technology picked up its pace to never before imagined levels, and media was becoming increasingly prominent in people's lives. During and before that time, lies and inaccuracies about Creation on both sides of the Creation versus evolution debate were also being broadcast and promoted to the entire world without Truth being the reason for the quest in the debates.

Ever since the theory of godless evolution was promoted, the errors of the teachers who adhered to the church teachings, especially those of the protestant sects became pronounced in a very profound way. This was much like when Galileo released his findings. (There is a great deal about this found in *The Science of God Volumes* discussing the likely order of events of Creation and what Genesis One actually says. The *The Science of God* books group the evens into general topics, such as physics of the heavens, biological aspects of life, and more. The book *Bending the Ruler* also discusses these topics but in a broader sense and more condensed manner.)

There is grave error from all sides in the debates surrounding the Creation topic, and neither side seems to realize their own errors. This would be a good place for all sides of this debate to take Christ's advice: "You hypocrite, first take the plank out of your own eye, and then you will see clearly to remove the speck from your brother's eye."

Yes, the errors of the Renaissance church precipitated the theory of evolution and the errors of evolution precipitated the exodus of the church. While Vatican II and Novus Ordo likely in some way contributed to the great Catholic exodus, it truly began centuries before that time, but it was not felt until around Vatican II and Novus Ordo during the cultural deviation of the mid-nineteen-hundreds.

Woe to you, Jesus said "If anyone causes one of these little ones—those who believe in me—to stumble, it would be better for them to have a large millstone hung around their neck and to be drowned in the depths of the sea." False teachers beware!, because the time is coming soon that your lies and deceptions will no longer be tolerated or accepted.

The establishment Catholic church holds little opinion regarding the details of the methods that the Creator God used to Create, so the Catholic church remained rather neutral in this matter only insisting that it is all God's handiwork *as it is stated in the Catholic Bible's Genesis One*. But even this neutral position carries with it some amount of responsibility. While modern telescopes are unquestionably useful in discerning the heavens, they in many ways are not needed to decipher Genesis One, but they do help to solidify it.

The problem with the Catholic church not having solid testable answers is that someone with opposing base views can concoct any illogical theory that *sounds* logical and promote it as "fact", and if there are no logical answers to combat it and expose its inaccuracies, then the opposing not-so-factual "facts" will be accepted and thus will deceive the congregation because the Catholic church shepherds had no solid answers to offer the people. Sadly, it was a Catholic priest who concocted the absurd expansion of the heavens theory which eventually came to be known as the "big bang theory". This illogical creation theory was initially proposed as being the manner in which God created the heavens. This alleged "science-based" theory has been embraced and then hijacked by the secular world but in a manner that is completely void of God. (If you have interest in this subject and why it is incorrect it is recommended that you look at the *The Science of God, Volumes 1 through 4* that dive deep into the Creation topic, as well as *Bending The Ruler*.) The church hierarchy will have a great deal of explaining to do on their judgement day when answering why the shepherds did not protect the flock from the ravenous wolves.

Most of the evolution theories were caused due to the protestant sect of the church as a result of their perversion of the Genesis Creation account text that is now printed in most of their Bibles. You can read why the protestant wing of the church is greatly responsible for the perpetuation of the evolution theory in more detail in the book *Understanding The Bible*. Change is good, but only when that change brings us all closer to the Spirit of Truth.

Chapter 15

Are All Churches the Same?

Let's elaborate a bit on the breakup of the Catholic church during the Reformation era. Change is good when it brings us closer to Truth, even if that change is breaking up the family for a time. Like it or not, this fragmentation within the church has in many ways strengthened the Bible during the *"Our-God-NO-our-God"* tug-of-war. Let's all recall here that this universal church was the **only** Christ-based church in its early days, but truth be told, fragmentation actually began almost immediately as can be read in the epistles where Saul-Paul was at odds with someone at the end of Acts Ch 15:39 "And there arose a dissension, so that they departed one from another; and Barnabas indeed taking Mark, sailed to Cyprus. But Paul choosing Silas, departed, being delivered by the brethren to the grace of God." This fragmentation got so bad after many years that the church elders decided to convene a counsel in the 300's AD to establish official church doctrine. From that point forward the church remained reasonably constant up until the events that precipitated the Reformation era.

But it is not all bad. Though it was sad to have any division within the church occur at all, God, in God's typical manner, made good come out of bad. Take for instance the Bible. The Bible has been translated many times over in recent centuries. But before that it was very constant with limited scrutiny. However, once the printing revolution began and the Reformation was underway the *Our-God-NO-our-God* tug-of-war began along with it. With the Bible being the rope that was being pulled from multiple ends, no side would dare have the others have the Bible as their own authoritative version, so each faction proceeded to deeply study the Bible and translate it to make theirs most accurate version by going back to the oldest known documents to be used as their source material. This was truly a gift to the world because as each group sought to create the most accurate translation, they unknowingly created a check-system that would prove to be very compelling as to what the majority of the Bible truly says and means.

As discussed in detail in *Understanding The Bible*, there are nuances and minor discrepancies in the various authoritative Bibles, but those discrepancies are few and minor. Additionally, the translation trail is far shorter than we tend to imagine it. There are, however, some very dubious more modern translations that are not fit for Bible study. Those versions will convey the general premise of Salvation, but when it comes to the pickier details of perhaps Creation and the theory of evolution, then they may as well be tossed in the trash. To better understand this, take a look at the books *Understanding The Bible* and *The Science Of God series*, you won't be disappointed. As a result, we find that the older authoritative Bibles are nearly identical in content and meaning and the doctrine extracted from those Bibles is similarly identical outside of the manmade rules that have been injected into that doctrine.

Duplicates Within

When you study the various Bibles, such as the Anglican King James Bible, The Catholic English Douay Rheims Bible, and the German Luther Bible, you will find them to be all in one accord. If you were blindfolded and were sitting in a church of any of the three primary sects during the mass part, you would be hard-pressed to tell which church you were in, unless you were very familiar with each of them. A person who does not attend mass on a regular basis or who has not attended mass for a long time would be unable to discern which is which. Yes, these universal sects are still in fact one Church, though many of us are too blind to see that this is so.

Do All Agree?

While the Catholic church gets a bit uppity about who is allowed to receive certain sacraments, and has its own idiosyncrasies, each church has strong prejudices against the others. The animosity that Lutherans have towards Catholics is really quite strong, but not so much in the other direction; yet you can find some animosity in the Catholic church towards Lutherans, but in that case it tends to be more within the individual members of the congregation, rather than in the congregation as a whole. Regarding the Lutherans, them teaching that "Catholics are wrong" is a part of their parochial education, at least while those schools still existed it was. The schools basically taught: "Catholics are wrong."

Then you have the battle between the Anglican church and the Catholic papacy. The Anglican Church of England has a borne-in resistance to the Catholic papacy as a part of their rebellion DNA through King Henry the VIII's rejection of the Pope. In fact, other religions also reject the Catholic church by reason of rejecting the papacy.

Interestingly, it is not the fundamental doctrine of the Catholic church that has caused the rift between the various sects. Much of the rift is derived due to the idea of papal "primacy". Churches simply do not want to be under the thumb of any one single supreme ruler who is an appointed typical-human leader. This goes back to the Reformation and the reason it came about. The people, many of them, simply did not like what the Pope of that time was doing, plain and simple there's not much more to it.

Are All People Universally Welcome In the Catholic Church?

Since the "Catholic church" means "universal congregation", is everyone welcome? Yes and no. The perversion of the church is not a good thing and will continue while wolves in sheep's clothing shepherd the flocks. If you recall in a previous chapter, we discussed the base-meaning of "Catholic", and found it to be "universal", not universal regarding people, but rather universal in regard to the teachings. **Everyone** is welcome to be a follower of those teachings, and so all who agree with and will follow the teachings and want to learn more about them are welcome into the Catholic church. This is similar with the Lutheran and Anglican sects of the universal church; they will welcome you in if you agree with *their* doctrine.

A little secret of the doctrine and dogma of these churches is that they mostly agree throughout. In other words, if you know the catechism or doctrine and dogma of one of them you pretty much know the catechism and doctrine and dogma of the others. With the unfortunate emphasis placed on their petty manmade differences, rather than on the universal alignment that they all share, the division continues. And because of this blindness, when they do come together again one day you must be alert, because they very possibly will come together as a one world church, rather than as the One True Church of Christ. If they do come together again they are likely to loosely follow the convoluted manmade doctrine of Saul-Paul, rather than the Pure

Truth of Jesus The Christ. Beware and watch for this as it begins to happen so that you do not get caught in its snare. "And Jesus answered and said unto them, Take heed that no man deceive you. For many shall come in my name, saying, I am Christ; and shall deceive many."

Orthodoxy

Orthodoxy is basically the commonly accepted practices and doctrine of a group. In the case of the various universal sects, it is their catechism that binds each. While each sect's catechism has differences from the others in arrangement and specific content, they are all referred to as "catechism" and the underlying key points are at one, which is to say "universal". But orthodoxy goes further with one aspect of orthodoxy being culture.

Culture is an unspoken sort of orthodoxy that is neither written nor said, but rather, it is lived. It is the orthodoxy that we live that truly dictates our future. It does not matter if it is a culture of the church or if it is worldly culture, because in truth it is all the same. You cannot go to church on Sunday and be all pious, but then on Monday go about living in ways that are contradictory to the church orthodoxy. This is a form of disassociated reasoning. We see this sort of thing quite often in politics where they pretend to want to "reduce the deficit" but then spend more wildly each succeeding year and somehow claim that they "fixed the problem" that they will again claim that they will fix the next congressional session.

The Catholic church made changes to the church doctrine during Vatican II when implementing Novus Ordo. The Novus Ordo doctrine stripped out important reverent detail from Liturgical prayers for the Catholic Liturgy. This ravaging of the doctrine of the Catholic liturgy caused a long-lasting rift in the Catholic church. This doctrinal schism brought about many new things to the church in effort to make the mass more "understandable" to the people because it was now being spoken in their regional native tongue. This sounds good, but the removal of much important points in the Liturgical prayers stole away a great deal of meaning from the Liturgy. Will this Liturgy ever revive from the amputations so recklessly done? Only time will tell. There are many people who are trying to re-establish the more reverent Latin mass in its entirety. But the Vatican and bishops forced them to stop, sometimes by closing those churches. This caused people and priests to take it upon themselves to find places to do the Liturgy in the way it was said and done before Vatican II's Novus Ordo was implemented.

These groups want the old reverent orthodoxy back in all of its glory. Should they fight the changes that now long ago occurred, or should they acquiesce to the demands of the Vatican and submit to the Vatican II Novus Ordo? Here we must ask ourselves, does it matter? And if so, then what is worse: to be unified and wrong, or to be separate and correct regardless of which side a person is on?

Full-Communion

Full-communion is the agreement between different churches' doctrine as discussed in the previous sections. Yet there is no particular set of doctrinal points that are specifically published and agreed upon, so the views on this are somewhat different between universal sects regarding what exactly constitutes "full-communion".

When churches are in full-communion, then the members can take part in the other churches' sacraments. Thus if you are a Catholic you can generally attend any Catholic church and receive the sacrament as you normally would while attending your home Church. With regard to the Catholic church and the divergent sects, it is time that the petty infighting ends. The animosity that the protestant sects have towards the Catholic church should have healed by now—it's been over a half a millennia! We need to move beyond the Reformation. Some of the changes desired by Martin Luther had been made long ago by the Catholic church, and it is now time for the sects to make amends and be at one in Truth.

The Catholic iron-fisted doctrine need only the slightest change to fill its pews full every weekend if only they could get over themselves regarding a few doctrinal points. The Catholic church could even bring back the Latin tradition to the mass with all of its details and it could be done in either the sacred Latin or in the native language of the region's people for each congregation, using the same words but in a different language. Further, the Pope could still exist as the ultimate church body arbiter, but the decisions could come from the bottom up and then be approved by the pope, rather than it being "the pope said so".

When the petty infighting finally ends and each sect shuts their mouths long enough to listen to—and hear and consider—the concerns of the other sects, we would quickly be in full communion. There's a great deal of arrogance in all of the universal sects, where the authoritarian nature of the hierarchy all are too pompous to admit to their failures—and every one of them have failures—lots of them! We are all stuck with this until we the people stand up for Truth in our churches. There is no reason that a Lutheran, Anglican, or Catholic should not be able to receive Holy Communion in each other's church. If everyone would pull their heads out of the sand and swallow their massive egos, they would see that we are in fact in full-communion even though we pretend otherwise. However, we are not necessarily in full-communion as a bride with The Christ.

At this point you have to look to Jesus The Christ and ask yourself, what do you imagine Jesus is thinking about the nonsense that is occurring between the people of the various church sects? Some teachings of the Catholic church are inconsistent with the statements made by many priests and pastors. Is Holy Communion required or not in order to get to Heaven? If it is, then does it have to be Catholic communion? If it does, then does that mean that all Anglican and Lutherans are going to go to hell? Again, what do we imagine Jesus would say about these Pauline things? There are similar thoughts from the other sects about the "Catholics" as well.

The degree to which each sect has animosity towards their sister sects is not necessarily about doctrinal issues. These tensions have been passed down through generations and it varies from person to person. So, the level of animosity each person has is going to be based upon their upbringing, their teachers, and their pastor or priest's instructions. The greater church will remain trapped in its insolence until the sects finally make amends, but I fear that before this occurs it will be too late and they will no longer be able to repent of, or prevent, their errors.

The clock is ticking more and more rapidly with each passing day—The time to repair relations is now! But, as mentioned in a previous section, **beware!** There will be efforts to form a *one world church* that many will mistake for the True Church of The Christ. Know Truth, "For this was I born, and for this came I into the world; that I should give testimony to the Truth. Every one that is of the Truth, hears <u>*my*</u> voice." Did you get that part? Jesus The Christ said <u>**MY Voice**</u>, not the Pope's, not Saul-Paul's, not some priest's, and certainly not the world's voice.

Chapter 16

Behold, a New Church

You might have noticed what would seem to be inconsistent grammar and capitalization in this book regarding the "church", but other than a few possible oversights, it is very deliberate. There is only one "Church" and there is no such thing as religion in the way we think of it today. This is where the Pauline doctrine needs to be flushed from the church. Saul-Paul was merely a preacher and should not carry the same weight in your heart as the twelve Apostles do, and the twelve Apostles should not carry the same weight in your heart as Jesus The Christ does.

Let us all get our priorities straight here. The entirety of the True Church is all about Original Sin and the Promise made to Adam and Eve by God, that through Adam and Eve's righteous offspring God would send The Word to save them. That Word was made Flesh and was embodied in Jesus The Christ. Jesus was beaten and then Crucified and died, went to hell to nullify the contract Adam and Eve unwittingly made with Satan, and then He Rose from the Dead and finally Ascended to Heaven—End of story! And if you reject that you have rejected Truth, which will prove to be problematic for you in the long-run.

The problem for mankind is that we can decide to believe or not to believe, but regardless of what we choose to believe, it does not change the Truth of what is true. There are additional concerns we still fail to see even if we all believe and follow Truth and actually finally come to realize that we are already in full-communion with most of our sister sects. Most religions have outreach programs to spread the Gospel, but can you imagine how much more could be accomplished if the universal sects were of one accord? Just consider the time and resources that are wasted due to the petty infighting—petty infighting which is **not** based on Christ's Words, but rather is caused by man's rules. Does this not feel wrong to you?

Do You See what I See?

I see a fractured church that is broken up into estranged sects who are constantly bickering and pointing fingers, and none are exempt. I reject these sects because they reject Christ. If Christ was writing this, Christ would say something to the order of: My True Church is not this sect or that sect, My True Church is those who follow My Word. "There is no more and no less than this, 'And thou shalt love the Lord thy God with all thy heart, and with all thy soul, and with all thy mind, and with all thy strength: this is the first commandment. The second is this: Love your neighbor as yourself. There is no commandment greater than these.'", and then Jesus The Christ would turn over our perverted alters and chase us out of his temples.

Hark! The Herald Angels Sing

The angels that heralded in The Christ Child did not speak so that any one particular sect could claim religious supremacy through their petty authoritarianism. If the Pope was truly sitting in the seat of Simon-Peter, he would be down on his knees publically washing the feet of the Cardinals, Bishops, and Priests like The Christ did who told his Apostles to do likewise. But has this been happening over the centuries? Not likely. The Cardinals, Bishops, and Priests should be following the example of Christ. There is little that anyone can say that will convince me that all of the leaders in each petty sect are following Christ's ways. Remember this little thing: "Beware of false prophets, who come to you in sheep's clothing, but inwardly they are ravenous wolves. You will know them by their fruits." As mentioned more than once in this book, the church ebbs and flows, it goes through good times and bad times. When there is vast sin within the church and abominations are set up in the temples that cause desolation of the temples, then what sort of fruit do *you* see that as? Is the tree bearing any good fruit?

"Do not be afraid. I bring you good news that will cause great joy for all the people. Today in the town of David a Savior has been born to you; He is the Messiah, the Lord. This will be a sign to you: You will find a baby wrapped in cloths and lying in a manger"

And

"Glory to God in the highest; and on earth peace to men of good will."

Do men of "good will" divide and separate? Do they scatter their flocks? Do they set up abominations that cause desolation? Now might be a good time for the clerical-wolves to go back to Bible class 101 and learn to be sheep again, rather than the wolves that far too many of them have become.

What Child is This

A couple of thousand years back a Child was born as the ultimate embodiment of The Holy Word of God. This Child came to break the gates of hell for the Salvation of any who would believe and repent. The Babe was not born so that we could separate and back-bite. The universal sects need someone to come along and smack their heads together, though, in their arrogance they would likely shout "SORRY!" at each other and then go stomping off and sulk and go right back to their same old divisive antics.

What Child is This? This Child is Jesus The Christ:

The Lamb

The Lamb of God

The Son Of Man

The Son Of God

The Word Made Flesh

The Word Of God

Redeemer

Savior

And

Salvation

Our Lord

Lord of Hosts

King of Kings

The Way

The Truth

And

The Life

Here we have the ultimate Promise, and they're worried about petty human rules, huh? Clergy, it's time to move on and join the True Church of Christ. Christ's True Church is not you clergy, it is the people, it is we the congregation of Christ!

Will we imagine that the Creator of the Universe is going to send The Word to us to save us when we can't even get along with our fellow man, especially as it pertains to *His* Kingdom? Many of the religions and various sects have a point in their words, but their actions show otherwise. Don't preach to the people about love and harmony and then allow division between universal sects.

The Christ told Simon-Peter that he would establish His Church upon Peter. He **did not say** the He would establish his

Church**es** upon Peter. And further, he likely said something closer to *Ecclesia* rather than "Church". Christ's *Ecclesia* is the congregation or people–it is his followers. So without perverting or stretching things we can easily surmise that that Christ would establish his following upon Simon–Peter. He was not referring to some authoritarian organization that would diminish His Truth and slowly replace it with the rules of man–Rules of man that all of the universal sects have foolishly fully adopted.

In the Bible it says "My people perish for lack of knowledge." Read your Gospels laity and clergy, you are ***not*** following The Good Shepherd. A Good shepherd will leave his flock to retrieve a single lost sheep. Yet each year more and more sheep are getting lost. Thus there are only few Good Shepherds remaining in the various church sects. We the congregation are also shepherds of those who are lost around us. Will we go out to seek those lost sheep? Or will we knowingly let them be consumed by the wolves?

If you recall, The Christ Said "Do you think I came to bring peace on earth? No, I tell you, but division. From now on there will be five in one family divided against each other, three against two and two against three. They will be divided, father against son and son against father, mother against daughter and daughter against mother, mother-in-law against daughter-in-law and daughter-in-law against mother-in-law." So I suppose it is fitting that the sects are divided. The problem for the sects is that the division Christ was speaking of was between those who follow his commands and those who don't follow. Be very careful here clergy, because many of you are treading a very fine line. Try to silence those speaking Truth if you will, but doing so never turns out well for those who deny Truth.

What Child is this? He is The Living Word of The One and Only Creator God who was sent to save the righteous repentant of the children of Adam and Eve, ***which happens to include the entire world of those who choose Truth of repentance***.

Chapter 17

Massive Sharing

There is great misunderstanding and ignorance regarding religion and the church. In the Old Testament it says, "My people perish for lack of knowledge" and Christ said "forgive them father for they know not what they do." There are blind wolves in the churches who seek to destroy the True Church body, but in their blindness both wolf and sheep wander to and fro at the edge of disaster. For we have forgotten our purpose.

Do this In Remembrance of Me

At Jesus The Christ's Last Supper, The Christ took some bread and he broke it, and said to his Apostles, "This is my body given for you; do this in remembrance of me." Later after supper, He took a cup of the fruit of the vine and said "This cup is the new covenant in my blood, which is poured out for you."

Can *remembering* Christ entail sin and not following Christ's ways? Can a divided church stand? No and no. We are seeing the end results of defying The Living Word of God, and it is not good.

Share the Information

And He said to them: "Go ye into the whole world, and preach the gospel to every creature." Also "Then Jesus came to them and said, 'All authority in heaven and on earth has been given to me. Therefore go and make disciples of all nations, baptizing them in the name of the Father and of the Son and of the Holy Spirit, and teaching them to obey everything I have commanded you. And surely I am with you always, to the very end of the age.'"

Did you get that part "teaching them to obey everything *I* have commanded you"? Regarding the mission of the Christ's True Church, there is perhaps no task more important than this. In the four Gospels we read accounts of Christ's Words to mankind, and those to whom he spoke were instructed to "Go ye into the whole world, and preach the gospel to every creature." The book of Acts and the Epistles tell us of some of the preaching done by the eleven original Apostles along with the newly selected Apostle Matthias as well as other followers, and also Saul-Paul the Pharisee. They would share the Good News information in the face of threats of imprisonment and death. It was not long before these threats became reality. In the bigger picture it was almost immediate that some were imprisoned, and not long after one was even stoned to death. Some died early in their mission, where others managed to avoid the wrath of fools and live much longer lives, thus enabling them to continue preaching to the world.

As the Good News was spread abroad by them, it ignited an unquenchable flame that those who opposed them could not quench. While the domineering authoritarian leaders lied and cheated and killed to slow the Apostles' progress, they could not stop the ever increasing momentum of Truth. Truth will always be deeply embedded within the hearts of The Christ's True Church. When needed, Truth will remain silent, and then when the time is proper The Word will flow out in a torrent of Truth that the world can no longer hide.

An interesting part of the great commission to Christ's followers is, "Go ye into the whole world, and preach the gospel to every creature." Did you get that, "to every creature"? This particular statement puts almost everyone in the category of *falling short of the mission given us by The Christ.* How many preachers and teachers and pastors and priests teach us to go and "preach the gospel to <u>every creature</u>"? And how many do it alone by themselves? Very few I suspect.

The Mass is Ended, Go In Peace?

There is a part of the ceremony when we attend church that is utterly missed by almost all of the congregation. When we go to church we are supposed to be witnessing the death and Resurrection of The Christ who is The Living Word during what is often referred to as the "Mass" or the "Liturgy". You might find it interesting that *Lit-urgy* is *lit, lith, laos* meaning "people or public" and *urgy* meaning "work". Thus the liturgy is *the work of the people*. And *Mass* means to "send". So when they say "the Mass has ended go in peace" it is really a misunderstanding of what is actually occurring or is intended to occur.

We typically attend "Mass" so very selfishly. Most people attend mass for their own salvation, in order to accept Christ in a tangible form, believing that The True Spirit of The Word of God becomes present upon the blessing and offering of the Bread and Wine. So, people come to receive this so that their "souls may be healed". Of course there's nothing wrong with this, but that is not really the entire purpose of the "Liturgy of the Mass". Mass never ends and will continue as will the Liturgy, until we are instructed by The Christ that it is no longer needed.

The True Church of Christ needs to hear and understand that the intent is not for the Salvation of *your* soul. That is a done deal if you live according to The Christ's words. The "Mass" is a part of "The Great Commission" and if you have ever attended a "Mass" then you automatically have become a part of that Commission. As a language-technicality, we don't attend a "Mass", rather it is the Liturgy Service that we attend and then we are to "Mass" or to go out and share the Liturgy.

The People's work, which is supposed to encapsulate the fundamental truths of our Salvation, is the "Liturgy" when we attend church services. This means that what occurs during the Liturgy is our work. Okay, we are supposed to do that which occurs during the Liturgy. I suppose we do this when we take part and receive communion, but that is the selfish part.

The Liturgy is considered the "people's work" because we are sent as implied in the term "Mass". So the sign-off at church should not be "The Mass is ended go in peace", it should be the Liturgy is your work and it is complete and I mass (or send) you, now "Go ye into the whole world, and preach the gospel to every creature." And if you are a part of the True Church of Christ, then that is what you will do through your every action. You live it and you speak of it as you live your life.

Chapter 18

The Desire of God

When you pause long enough to consider the vastness of Creation and the overwhelming beauty therein, it is nearly impossible to miss the fact that God's only desire for us is good. Sometimes people say that God never destroys, but this is fool's-speak. Of course God has destroyed things, but only to remove corruption and rebuild things with a hopefully better and more faithful people, much the way we will tear down a decrepit building to make way for a new stronger and better one. If you are paying close attention, this should give you a clue as to what will happen to the universal sects if they do not promptly clean up their act. Although, that is unlikely to happen due the human arrogance and our defiance of God and of God's Truth, and this defiance has been practiced within most universal sects in recent decades and in recent centuries.

The Harvest

Jesus spoke of "harvest" on more than one occasion. He also indicated that there would be weeds or "tares" sown within the crops. But He implied that we are not to burn the entire crop to remove the weeds. Instead we are to let it all mature until the time of harvest and then pluck out the weeds and cast them into the fire because then they are more easily identified. That time is drawing near. The question is, are you and your words weeds? Or are you and your words a part of the actual crop?

Our Desire

God's desire is for us to wake up and to see the light of Truth and accept it and allow it into us and to embrace it and to never let it go. But what is **our** desire? Do we desire that? Do we desire Truth? The quick answer to that is, yes! Every one seeks Truth but when no one has taught them that Truth exists or the methods of Truth, then they will tend to go wayward. Drugs, alcohol, random sex, bodily mutilation and marking, and most other vices are all attempts to fill the void where Truth is meant to be within you. So we don't just have a desire for Truth when we finally figure things out, our desire for Truth is inherent in every single human being from the moment we are conceived onward.

When we understand that we live in Satan's dominion, it becomes far easier to see that there is a constant assault against us in effort to push us off track and distract and confuse us so that we don't ever look towards the Light of Truth. Light has this interesting effect where even the slightest glimmer lights up an entire room and the more of a glimmer that enters the room then the more easily you can spot the lies that are keeping you from the light. So as you can see, it is obviously in Satan's best interest to keep the distractions coming at us at an ever increasing pace as we each get closer to the Light. This is because when someone truly sees the Real Light of Truth they will seldom go back to their old way of life. The religious labels such as "Catholic" or "Lutheran" etc. are mere distractions that Satan uses to keep the Light of Truth hidden from us, because it takes our focus off of The Christ.

Taking Action

How do we take action? Must every person go out and preach to all of the world? Not necessarily. We are to, above all, receive Truth, and if you have not come to a point that you are at one with Truth, then be very careful with your words, because if you preach error and lead others astray by you yourself being a blind sheep without Light, then you make yourself to be a false preacher. You are then "The blind leading the blind." Remember this statement that The Christ made in Mark 9:41: "whoever causes one of these little ones who believe in Me to sin, it would be better for him if a millstone were hung around his neck, and he were drowned in the depth of the sea."

To take action, you first need get to know Truth above all else. Love Truth with all of your heart, all of your mind, and all of your soul. In saying this we are not to understand this as some nonsensical "your truth or my truth" sort of deception. There is only one Truth and if you will not seek it, you will never find it. "Ask and it will be given to you; seek and you will find; knock and the door will be opened to you. For everyone who asks, receives; the one who seeks finds; and to the one who knocks, the door will be opened." Truth was primarily what the Christ was speaking of, and from it, much good will come to you.

Children and Family

Seeds multiply with each generation. Look to plants that produce the various grains, you place a single kernel of corn into the ground and from it springs several cobs of corn with each containing hundreds of kernels. Then you plant those in the ground and you quickly get a great deal of kernels. Now take several generations of this and your storehouses cannot contain the harvest. It is similar with the children of a married couple. For people who love and have children it only takes four or five generations to have over a hundred descendants. For some people it is even less. So ask yourself this: what is your desire for those children? Do you want them having sexual relations on par with the "sexual revolution" with them being intimate with many people and then hating themselves for doing so, so much so that they hate the babies produced from those illicit unions to a point where they want to kill their own children with abortions and end up diseased as well? Or do you want them to find someone to truly love and care for them and produce kind and loving grandchildren that you also can teach and offer love to?

There are not a whole lot of options here; you either remain completely alone, or you have relations with many people in effort to fill the unquenchable abyss of a void that is in your life, or you select the alternative option and patiently seek one loving lifelong mate with whom you are able to produce offspring and bring a family up for the Glory of God, or maybe adopt children who were produced by the empty souls seeking to fill their own void with sexual intimacy. This is where removing some of the reverence in the Liturgy may have indirectly also taught irreverence in general, including in relationships. The irreverence of Novus Ordo and the irreverence of the "sexual revolution" do coincide, so there may be a vague legitimate connection.

This is one of those areas of thought where we need to decide as to whether or not we each will accept the fact that there truly is a Creator God who spoke all things into existence. **Remember** that we get to decide what we will choose to believe about anything, <u>but we **do not** get to decide what is true</u>, this is because what is true is true whether it or not we believe it. This is true whether or not the "Creator God" actually exists. What is true is true and what is not true is not true no matter how badly we might want and hope something to be otherwise. As mentioned earlier, we are all born filled with Truth, but that Truth is beaten out of us as we age, thus leaving an abyss of a void within us.

When we are not brought up in a loving environment overflowing with Truth, we then struggle and attempt to fill that void with anything that feels good to us. Create a loving environment overflowing with Truth for your children so that

Truth flows into them at all times. Your children are your seeds with which to feed the world. They will feed the world or at least their part of it no matter what. But what sort of fruit will **your** children produce? You are the tree and your children are the fruit, and you can tell a tree by the fruit it bears. What kind of tree are you?

The True Church and True Bride

The True Church of Christ is not the "Catholic church" or the "Lutheran church" or the "Anglican church" or any other church. All of these universal sects might believe nearly all of the same things, but not one has full claim and title to being Christ's True Church. It's true that the Roman Catholic church can trace the papal succession back to Simon-Peter, and this co-called "Catholic" church exists because of the Apostles preaching the Gospel. But this does not make the Catholic church Christ's True Church. The True Church is not some organization with an authoritarian hierarchy that leads the sheep astray like a wolf posing as a shepherd in a flock with no shepherd

The True Church is the Pure and Clean Bride of Christ. It is not the leaders, it is not the organization, it is not the Liturgy or the mass. There are many people within these universal sects who are indeed a part of the True Church, but that does not automatically make those labeled churches The True Church of Christ. You are *not* a body of the whole *at one* with God if you are following error, no matter how pure your intentions are.

The True Church of Christ is the True Bride of Christ and only those who follow **Christ's** commands and reject all others have made themselves a part of it. The bulk of the Liturgies in all of the universal sects are good and true, and the practice thereof is good. But just because criminals sometimes do good things, those good things do not alleviate their guilt when doing wrong.

So as to not cast away the wheat with the tares, we must not reject these universal sects, but rather bring them together to be *at one* in accord with Jesus The Christ's teachings and commands, and then remove the tares. Often when someone speaks against the church like Martin Luther did, those who are observing will misunderstand and rebel, thus completely leaving the church and starting their own sect—This is not right! What must be done is to protect the True practices of the universal church by implementing only Christ's teachings into the doctrine and removing all other incorrect teaching from that doctrine, and then use the purified doctrine to move forward as per the guidance of Simon-Peter.

Is papal authority good? Somewhat, but it is dangerous when a pope goes rogue. Popes do offer a central point of focus, but what is more important is that the True Congregation, which is the True Church, must at all costs maintain the True purpose of the Liturgical Mass to "Go ye into the whole world, and preach the gospel to every creature." Without this, Salvation will only be carried a single generation. It is the workers who pass the message of True Salvation down from generation to generation who are the True Church of Christ, along with, of course, those who adhere to that teaching after it has been shared with them.

Chapter 19

The Church Memory

In all that has been said in the previous chapter you should by now have picked up on the importance of keeping with an accurate set of standards that are taught to each successive generation so that they too can "Go ye into the whole world, and preach the gospel to every creature." When we fail to pass this on to subsequent generations, we fail those generations.

Retain what You Can

The basics of the death and Resurrection of The Christ are so common that they become cliche and mostly forgotten in our hearts and minds, only to be resurrected on key holidays. This is why it is important for most people to attend church on a somewhat regular basis. If we are paying attention to the church service, we are then reminded of both the Death and Resurrection of The Christ. Church services, that is to say the service of the congregation, are an enduring tradition that without, the likelihood that we today would even know about Salvation from The Christ while we are still alive is about zero.

You might question this because the Gospel and its effects are abundantly embedded nearly everywhere we look in society. In fact, this is so predominant that it is like the *Hot Water* spoken of earlier. It is so common that we don't realize that we're in it. People who travel the world and are paying attention will notice this to an extent when they experience non-universal church cultures, but most cultures have some bit of Christianity embedded in them and yet are unaware that this is so. This is to a point were some of these cultures attempt to take credit by stating that the ideas of Christianity came from their culture, rather than the other way around.

This unavoidable saturation is because of Christ's True Church doing the work of the Great Commission to "Go ye into the whole world, and preach the gospel to every creature." Without the universal church sects there to carry forward the Liturgy and Mass, the people would not have been sent out doing the work. It simply just would not have been there.

Always Remember Tradition

Tradition for some folks is old-fashioned nonsense, but without tradition you would not even be able to talk and communicate with your fellow man. Tradition can be a bad thing, but in general it has brought many advances throughout the world. If we did not have a tradition of language then the language would change so much with each generation that one generation would not be able to effectively communicate with a subsequent generation. The particular tongue and dialect of any region of the world is a language-tradition. If you chose to forget your language-tradition, which appears to be ever more common as years pass, then you will lose your culture and likely adopt a new culture that is unknown to your ancestors who offered their lives for your language and cultural traditions.

Truth is obviously more than a tradition, but the practice of Truth is only a tradition, and it was incumbent upon the True

Congregation of Christ to carry that tradition forward via "Go ye into the whole world, and preach the gospel to every creature." This is done in the Liturgy; it is your tradition and your work. Oddly enough, this activity has become so treasured and common that it is difficult to avoid nearly anywhere on Earth. When Novus Ordo stripped out key parts of this universal tradition, it did damage the church greatly. However, since the Liturgy Mass was being said in Latin, many people didn't really know the specifics anyway.

Some people blame the exodus from the Catholic church on the dubious implementation of Vatican II and the subsequent removal of the Latin service Mass and the insertion of Novus Ordo in its place. But as discussed in a previous chapter, the Catholic exodus was a long time in coming. The combination of post-Reformation textual perversion of Genesis One along with a Cultural Revolution of removing prayer from schools plus, the addition of the "Sexual Revolution" all coupled with the irreverent changes encapsulated in Vatican II with Novus Ordo ended by creating the perfect situation for Satan to quickly steal away the church.

When the schism happened with the Reformation rebellion fallout after Martin Luther took his stand with his ninety-five theses, it caused a tear in the very fabric of the universal church that perpetuated the exodus. While attendance of the congregation has always moved like a modern stock exchange chart with its ups and downs, the problem was largely hidden until the mid-twentieth century. The rebellion caused an undermining of tradition that slowly infiltrated nearly every one of the newly splintered universal sects. This undermining also became a tradition containing both evils and blessings.

Holidays

Not many people ponder words, such as "holiday". What is a holiday? Is the Fourth of July a holiday? Is New Year's Eve a holiday? "Holiday" is a "Holy Day". Holy Days are special days set apart that we are supposed to celebrate in remembrance of the stories contained in the Bible which are also connected to a True Liturgy, such as Christmas, and also Easter, or more accurately stated–Resurrection Day. Christmas is an easy holiday to understand. Christmas is *Christ-Mass* or Send the message of the arrival of Christ. We do this when we publicly acknowledge Christ. While it is sometimes done in selfish ways only for financial gain, we nonetheless promote Christmas and the Christmas message in a very big way internationally during the time of the year of its feast day–that is to say, Christmas Day.

And then "Easter" also promotes the Liturgical tradition internationally regardless of the word "Easter's" potential nefarious origins with its title's alleged ties to paganism. It is true that many people don't even realize that this is all occurring, but it is occurring and it is undeniably evident and nearly impossible to avoid, try as they might. No, we cannot avoid the deeply rooted Liturgical work of the people or the Mass from which it is sent. It is our culture, it is us, and nearly every good thing we have on Earth would not exist without those particular foundations of Liturgical holiday tradition.

These traditions have been carried through the ages by the Catholic church and the various sects thereof. As society continues in its current collapse, we see people working in vain to try to blot Christmas out of society by attempting petty censorship by using the term "x-mas". But the True Church tradition is buried so deeply into our world culture that even the "x" in x-mas bears the seal of the cross. It is a monumental task to learn the many nuances of Language translation, but there are some basic points to be made. Language is a tradition given to us by God. There are ancient letters, one of which is the *tau* or *tav* spoken of early in this book. That letter *tav* is a symbol of Truth and is the last letter of the Hebrew alephbet. It is shaped like a cross or "t" or an "x". So, as you can see with every word and utterance we make we are either raising ourselves up, or we are damning ourselves. We don't get to choose these things, they just are, and we either use them for our good, or to our destruction.

A Church Then and Now

Should the True Church ever change? That question can have complex answers, but the answer is yes and no depending upon what aspect we are talking about. It is of no concern to God if we serve God in our own way if it is in accord with Christ's words and commands, so yes these things can change without separating ourself from the True Church. But when it comes to the core of the Liturgy, it will never change. Sure we can foolishly strip out content like was done with the new mass referred to as Novus Ordo. But the True Liturgy is not something that man concocted, rather it is man's retelling the Promise God made to Adam and Eve and the fulfillment of the Promise through the Crucifixion, Death, Resurrection, and Ascension of Jesus The Christ. So, while we can lie and change the story or leave important parts of it out of our liturgies, the one True Liturgy can never change, not ever, because *it is history*. That is to say that the people's work to tell the full true story of Salvation will never change. The True Liturgical message will always remain, and it is the work of every member of the True Church to "Mass", which is to be sent out to share that message.

Many deeply dedicated Catholics believe that the Novus Ordo Liturgy Mass is the reason society had gone into a dangerous decline around the turn of the twentieth century, but it was not the cause—Novus Ordo is a *result*. There is nothing wrong with returning to the reverence of the Latin Mass and the way in which it was done prior to Vatican II, and it would probably be a good thing to do so. But returning to the old Latin Liturgy will not solve the problem, it probably won't hurt anything, but it certainly is not going to fill the churches.

Earlier in this book, evolution was briefly mentioned. The idea of accidental spontaneous evolution is a childish approach to science that, intended or not, strips away the need for a Creator, but in our minds only.

When the Pope behaved in such a way as to invoke the sale of indulgences for the salvation of souls, it set off a series of events leading to the decline of the Catholic church. The devout Catholic priest Martin Luther was correct about Salvation not being able to be bought and sold, and the Catholic church's action against Martin brought on the Reformation revolt. This in turn coupled with the newfound Guttenberg printing press revolution allowed the Bible to be mass-produced more easily with each new innovative adaption to the printing press. Then due to the DNA of the protesting spawn of the Reformation, many new sects rebelled and "reformed" their own interpretation of the Bible.

With the ability to easily paraphrase and reprint the Bible, these new sects substituted their own interpretation of the Bible text to replace the original Bible text, which was and is particularly damaging in the Bible's Genesis One Creation account. The books *Understanding The Bible, Bending The Ruler,* and *The Science Of God series Volumes* explain the scientific and interpretation errors in order to correct the record in people's hearts and minds. The post-Reformation Genesis One translations were being done to help the common man make more sense of the text, but they failed miserably because the inaccuracies and misinterpretations thereof caused the members of these sects to believe what are essentially lies and inaccurate description of what actually occurred during Creation. This problem continues even in the modern scientific era.

You might be wondering, why is that such a big deal? It's because when the very first page, in fact the very first sentence, of the Bible is taught wrong with the full force of the particular religion, and then "science" comes along and offers additional erred "insight", it then undermines the Bible and supports the Biblical inaccuracies that those people where taught. This invalidates both the Genesis One Creation account **and** the Creator in people's minds, because Godless "science" appears to explain it better, thus making the Bible read like a fairytale. And since science is also wrong but appears to make a little more sense in understanding the formation of the universe, people end up altogether abandoning the Bible. At this point the Bible is foolishly being taught based upon dangerous blind faith alone.

Here's the horror of this slaughter of faith; The Catholic church didn't really hold all that strong of an opinion on the Creation topic. The Catholic church simply implies that Creation was done according to the Genesis One Creation account (in the Catholic Bible), the church might not fully understand it, but acknowledges that Genesis One is the account of the Creation events. That's all well and good, but with the later post-Reformation Bibles being mass-produced by these new religious sects, no matter how well-meaning they were, those terribly incorrect interpretations have filtered into society at an alarming pace. These erred Creation accounts worked their way into the hearts and minds of many who were and are a part of the Catholic church.

As the post-World War II generation grew (referred to as the "Baby Boom generation") and was put into public schools, prayer was deemed "unconstitutional" in the schools. This would never have occurred had the Bible not been undermined by shoddy translation efforts done by modern reformers. These students were then told that the Bible is "wrong and is just a bunch of stories", which was due to those erred Bible translations. The liability sits on the shoulders of those who created those erred translations as well as on those who teach from those Bibles. There is much blood on the hands of those false translators and false teachers. As it says in Mark, "whoever causes one of these little ones who believe in Me to sin, it would be better for him if a millstone were hung around his neck, and he were drowned in the depth of the sea."

Sometimes people want to pin the blame on Martin Luther, but please keep in mind that while he was a unique individual, it was the church at that time that would not recant of their lies. And further, please take note that the Early Anglican King James

Bibles and the Early German Luther Bibles and the Early English Catholic Bibles were all authoritative well-translated Bibles. Maybe not to perfection, but all are very close in nature. The same cannot be said of a slew of other late post-reformation Bible versions that were printed after that time. But I digress.

The Baby Boom generation was the first generation to be influenced in their home with television sets. They were also the recipients of ever-increasing availability of books and very tightly constructed education promoting evolution. As these children aged, they saw lots of imagery and read books that promoted the theory of evolution in the face of the flawed translation attempts of the Bible's Creation account. These two *origin* accounts do not reconcile. So unless the person had a great amount of blind faith, they gradually slipped away from the foundation of the Bible and gravitated to the more logical-sounding big bang and evolution theories.

Then as that generation grew older and their hormones were raging in the sixties, they went wayward. In the midst of all of this, the Catholic church was watching the beginning of the societal freefall during the adolescence of the Baby Boom Generation, and then in an attempt to address this international problem they convened Vatican II and through unscrupulous means Novus Ordo was contrived. Novus Ordo certainly did not help the situation, in fact it was a final slap in the face to many people who did not like the rapidly changing culture that was increasingly drifting away from God.

With the reverence of the old Latin Mass now lost and the Bible undermined by far too many horrible late-post-Reformation translations, and the sexual revolution of a generation who had their foundation crumble beneath them, it all led to the near death of the Catholic church. Yet within all of that Jesus Christ's True Church still dwelt.

The difference between the True Church of Simon-Peter's time and the modern Church of the twentieth and twenty-first centuries is that their Biblical foundation had not been perverted with horribly translated versions of the books of the Bible back then. Nor did they have the epistles of Saul-Paul to be the tares in their wheat. The reason that the True Church grew so rapidly in the past centuries is because all of mankind is seeking to fill the void within ourselves with the Light of Truth. That is what we were created for—to be vessels of Light and to shine that Light for all to see for the Glory of God. In the early days of the Church there was far less calculated premeditated deception occurring.

The following might seem to contradict the church and the Bible, but it does not. It is probably a good thing that people are leaving the church, because regardless of what is being taught in the church, if the people believe inaccurate accounts of the Bible they will more easily be led astray by those wolves who misguide and ravage the blind sheep. The departure is probably good and should probably continue until the universal sects all see the errors of their doctrine and teaching, and then correct it to realign it all with Truth. And when that happens, the churches will then automatically begin to overflow once again. Since we are vessels Created to be filled with Truth, it makes perfect sense that people would eventually leave any church that is teaching lies and inaccuracies about our origins and morality.

Truth is not the opposite of lies. Truth is the opposite of anything that is not true. A lie is the deliberate intent to deceive, where inaccurate information, on the other hand, is not. So when people retranslated the Bible in their own understanding, they might have done so with good intent, but when something is incorrect then then it is not in alignment with what actually occurred. God made us in the Image of God, but we try to make the Bible in the image of us—but it is not. The Church of Simon-Peter's time was closer to Truth than the Catholic church sects are in our modern era. However, almost immediately after Saul-Paul's conversion Saul-Paul had disagreements causing rifts in the early church, so in that respect with the modern church, it is unfortunately "business as usual".

Chapter 20

The Church Identity

Everyone seeks to have an identity and to "find themselves". But this task has become increasingly difficult as we separate from our true foundation. In the book *Hot Water* there is much about our personal identity that ultimately relates to God, but what about The Christ's True Church's identity?

The Husband Compared to the Wife

The husband is to be likened to a priest and the wife a treasured temple. He enters into her to and offers himself to dwell within her. This is similar to the whole of God's Creation where God dwells within us. Due to some misunderstanding of the Biblical text, and especially the epistles, people in the modern era have deceived themselves to believe that priests should not get married. This has led to a lack good of shepherds in the church. To compensate for these priestly shortages, people foolishly seek to allow women to become priests.

In our foolish human nature we tend to make the wrong choices quite frequently, and often those choices come with deep and long-lasting ramifications. It is the fool's way to break from God's order and make women to be priests or to insist that priests are not to be married. Should all priests get married? Not necessarily; marriage should be a personal choice. There is nowhere in the Bible's True scriptures that it is implied priests should not be married.

There are many good priests out there, but there also many not so good priests out there. However, there are many very good married men who would warmly welcome the task of being a priest and shepherding the flock and doing the Liturgy of the Catholic Mass.

The solution to the priest problem is pretty simple; if you want to remain celibate then you should make the commitment to do so, and if you break that commitment then you should no longer be able to be a priest because it is as if you divorced God and replaced God with a woman in your vow to God. But if you want to marry a woman and be a priest, then when going into the agreement your commitment on earth is to that woman, and if you divorce her you should no longer be able to be a priest because you broke your commitment to her *and* to God. And in both cases if you have relations with someone other than who you have committed to then you are an adulterer and should be removed from being a shepherd of the flock and from being able to say the Liturgy of the Mass in church. It really is that simple. All other restrictions are man's rules.

Women should never be priests. The reason for this is the very blatantly obvious nature of our design. Now, I can imagine in modern culture that many women would get angry at that statement assuming that they have no say in any of this. But this is not true because neither men nor women have any say in this. The terms have been set several thousand years ago and even The Christ himself said "For I tell you truly, until heaven and earth pass away, not a single jot, not a stroke of a pen, will disappear from the Law until everything is accomplished." But let us step beyond this for a moment and revisit the women serving subject. The "Law" says that men are to be the priests, but does not bar women from speaking about God. So, it is okay for women to share the message of the Liturgy of the Mass and discuss it in public places in front of others, but that is different than actually performing the Liturgy in church and offering the Sacrifice.

The fact that the priestly tasks were placed on men rather than on women is not an affront to women, rather it actually serves to make women far more important and special than they and society have been making themselves out to be.

What We Represent

Mankind is made in the image of God as is indicated in Genesis One: "So God created mankind in his own image, in the image of God he created them male and female he created them." This is a clear indication of the likeness and level of equality of man and women. We are the same in value, we are equal in value. We represent God the Creator. We can create life that has intellect and can love in a way that unexplainably exceeds the animals. Within a committed relationship and with the help of a man's seed, a woman is Sanctified and Glorified for God, and because her womb is the temple sanctuary for the child that is Created within her, there is no greater task pertaining to "man" than that particular gift of woman, which is why abortion is so very heinous.

While those who bow to the god of evolution have some very interesting and compelling points, they fail to really put their finger on the difference between humans and animals which lends to their argument, but it does nothing to help anyone understand the obvious differences that we see. People can reason, and even animals can reason to some extent. People communicate and animals communicate. People can reproduce and animals can reproduce. But after hundreds of years of study into the possibility of evolution, from amoeba to man, no one has yet been able to offer a fully adequate natural explanation of why man is strikingly different than all animals. Spoiler alert: We are made in the image of God! We are not gods, but we are God-like in the image of God. We even know good from evil like God does. Not right from wrong, but rather Good from Evil, which is a very important distinction to be aware of.

Statues In the Likeness

The second of the Ten Commandments states "You shall not make for yourself an image in the form of anything in heaven above or on the earth beneath or in the waters below. You shall not bow down to them or worship them; for I, the Lord your God, am a jealous God." So what are the limits on this Commandment?

There is one clear limit and it is that we are to bow down and worship **only** The Creator God. Any other thing we worship violates this Commandment. But are there limits regarding "an image in the form of anything in heaven above or on the earth beneath or in the waters below"? For many people the jury is still deliberating that question. Some people are absolutists having no images allowed whatsoever, where others are okay with most images as long as we do not bow down and worship them. And to further refine the questions in this topic, what specifically constitutes an "image"? Is exposed photographic film an image? Is a picture in a magazine an image? Is a drawing an image? Is a sculpture an image? Is a moving or still picture on a TV or video screen and image? Is a statue an image?

It's risky for us to demand that God meant this or that particular thing about such images, but if it means that we are simply not to make *any* images whatsoever "in the form of anything in heaven above or on the earth beneath or in the waters below" then we are all in great peril and God duped us when the people made the Ark of the Covenant and were told to make images that were in the form of things in heaven above and on the earth beneath. So God either damned us with the Second Commandment and the subsequent making of the Ark of the Covenant, or we are misunderstanding that Commandment.

But it's right for us to question people kneeling before a statue of a saint or of Jesus' Mother Mary and praying before it. Sure we are supposedly praying to these people to be intercessors or intermediaries between us and God, but how do our actions appear to the onlookers when we do so?

While the statues may not be explicitly be in violation of the Second Commandment of their own accord, the difference between them being an acceptable image or becoming an idol is only the fine line within our hearts regarding our understanding and intention when we kneel and pray before such statues. This is something that we must be ever-aware of because that fine line has been crossed many times throughout human history while leading to the destruction of many civilizations that fell into Satan's idolatrous trap.

Judge Them by Their Works

Most people have heard the term "the apple doesn't fall far from the tree." This means that the fruit of the tree is like the tree and near to it, which is an adaption of Christ's statement "Ye shall know them by their fruit." As the societal generations evolve, the children of those who kneel before the statues will often adopt similar behavior. But unbeknownst to the parent, their example of kneeling may be reproduced but in a different setting with the focus no longer having affection towards God, but instead having affection towards the actual statue idol.

We see this problem unfolding in the modern era at an increasing pace. The urge to pray in front of a focal point of a statue or picture, has devolved into sitting many hours in front of an illuminated screen with moving images while serving those images and thinking about those images while we are completely devoid of any thoughts of God.

If our children misunderstand what might be in our heart, then they will not understand our actions and the way we intended those actions. This is a very common problem that most of us miss, and it is the source of most of the world's woes. It is by our outward example that our children learn from us, rather than by our internal and unspoken intent. And, unless we explain things to them or they happen to be extraordinarily aware children, we will lead them astray in doing such marginal activities regarding the Second Commandment.

Can You Be a Soldier for Christ When You Live In Sin?

You might not be living in sin if you kneel before a statue and pray to God or even the saint who you are asking to intercede for you, but your children very well may if they do not understand your internal mental actions. So if you are leading people, namely your children, astray in this way, then can you be a soldier for Christ? No you cannot. No matter how good your intentions are, if you happen to be causing people to get the wrong idea you are causing problems and may very well be the cause of their damnation in the end. There is no statue, and no trinket worn, and no bodily marking that will ever replace or even remotely compete with a true internal dedication to God and Christ's ways. Those items only serve as distractions to your True dedication to God.

When it comes to statues and their effects, you have to look to Christ's actions. Have you ever read *anything* in the Bible that Jesus The Christ did or asked us to do that was remotely close to kneeling and praying before any form of graven image or using any type of trinket as a reminder and focus? Not likely! True followers or soldiers of Christ are going to place above all the spiritual health of their fellow man. And if there is something that others see them do that is on the edge of sinning, then they will cease that activity if they are True Followers.

Primacy and Authority of the Pope

The actions of elders, such as parents, have deep and lasting ramifications on the children of that family. The same is true of popes. When a pope makes a mistake, or fails to correct mistakes that other leaders made, such as the excessive marketing and subsequent sale of indulgences, it can and likely will have long-lasting effects on the family as it did in that situation, eventually bringing on a rebellion and the subsequent Reformation and separation of the people. Everything we do matters, and the popes are especially culpable in their actions. This would not be so if not for the unjustified level of importance placed on that papal position, but they themselves make this so by claiming and adhering to "papal primacy".

The words of the Pope can put fear into the hearts of the people, or love into the hearts of people. True authority can only be had as a result of speaking in utter Truth. This is why Jesus The Christ spoke with Authority, and the other leaders of his time who wanted to speak with such authority were jealous of Him because they did not understand Christ's appeal or how He did it. They didn't have the ability to speak Truth because their own opinions about the scriptures placed a basket over their own lamps of Truth. Their own arrogant methods of teaching made them fail in comparison to The Christ.

Authority is not something that is passed down from one person to the next so as to imagine that Truth is somehow conferred from one pope to the next. Authority is granted to man only through the Spirit of Truth, and no man has primacy over any other man. We do however create inferiority within ourselves when we deny Truth. If we do deny Truth, it does not make others better than we are, rather, it makes us less than we were meant to be. While the others remain the same as they were, *we* choose to lower ourselves. No man, including the Pope, is better than any other and therefore technically has no "primacy" over others. The Popes are not better or smarter than others, and in many cases, some popes were far worse than most people. Anyone who has chosen to deny Truth has lowered themselves and placed themselves in great danger, including popes who fail to open themselves up to Truth

Peter 30 : Paul 212

Upon reading the Trent *Catholic Catechism for Parish Priests*, from which the modern Catholic Catechism is derived, it becomes increasingly disturbing with nearly every page read. Reading the catechism as a younger child will not have the level of meaning as when reading it as an adult. This is especially true if you are much older and more studied. When speaking of religious beliefs, people often get very protective at any words that they perceive as an attack on their religion. So if someone was to speak of anything in the Bible or in church doctrine that in any way whatsoever negatively views it or is even perceived negatively, they will often immediately take a viciously defensive position to protect their territory. This makes sense and it is good that they are willing to protect their beliefs, but only so long as those beliefs are actually grounded in Truth.

If one makes any attempt to correct things and remove focus from Saul-Paul's words and place the focus back on The Christ's words it has a tendency to make Saul-Paul's followers take that defensive position just mentioned in the previous paragraph. As discussed in a previous chapter, Saul-Paul was a Pharisee and if not for the real Apostles' disciple Ananias having a vision concerning Saul-Paul, Saul-Paul would have had no one to corroborate him. Placing Saul-Paul's writings in the proper place within our hearts and minds and within our understanding is the goal. In a rough counting of New Testament epistle quotes in the Catholic Catechism, Saul-Paul was found to have in excess of 210 references, and Simon-Peter, who is the rock upon which the Church was to be established, has roughly only 30 in the Catholic Catechism. Now to be fair, Saul-Paul has many more pages in the Bible than Simon-Peter does, but since Simon-Peter is the rock the church is said to be built upon, should it not be that it is only Simon-Peter's letters and letters from any of the other eleven Apostles that the catechism is based upon? After all, the church refers to itself as the holy Catholic and "Apostolic" church that is supposed to be established on Simon the rock. The Catechism often refers to the Pharisee Saul-Paul as "The apostle" when he really is not an official Apostle. But Simon-Peter is the key Apostle and is rarely quoted or referenced in comparison with Saul-Paul.

Further, the elaboration via opinion regarding Saul-Paul's writings surrounding the Saul-Paul quotes comprises a dominant portion of the *Trent Catholic Catechism*. This is true of the Modern Catholic Catechism as well, but in the Modern Catechism the Saul-Paul references are relegated to footnote citations, so it is considerably more difficult to detect this problem in the modern versions.

We must understand that Saul-Paul was little more than one of today's preachers. Over the years there has been no shortage of preachers that claim to have had visions or encounters such as Saul-Paul had but with differing content. This does not make Saul-Paul any more or less valid; it merely places him in the proper position of a *preacher*. Sadly as with many religious leaders, we tend to follow a leader rather than what the leader was trying to teach us to follow.

The Catholic church doctrine is far more built upon what Saul-Paul said than it is anything else. Of course it involves The Christ, but where Saul-Paul's words are concerned the interpretation of those words tends to take precedence in people's minds, largely due to the fact that Saul-Paul's words often dominate sermons heard in church-sect services and many other publications. This issue has been the cause of a great many troubles within the church and is partly responsible for the events leading up to and including the rebellion and Reformation. The universal church has its beliefs and its rules, many of which are good. But many of its problems come through misunderstanding and misinterpretation and subsequent perversion of Saul-Paul's convoluted epistles. We see this happen with other parts of the Bible as well, but those are usually very easily pointed out and rebutted, but it is not so with Saul-Paul's epistles. If you watch for this you will see it more and more as you become more aware of it. It is true that Saul-Paul's words have had some positive impact on the world, but even within Saul-Paul's own epistles, we can see the problems and confusion that his words caused for many of those to whom he wrote.

The Catholic church doctrine is rooted in Truth, but is erroneously done through the foundation of Saul-Paul. And the doctrine of the church is built upon that Pauline foundation, yes there are a few pieces of Simon-Peter in there, but not as many as ought to be in comparison. If not for verse where people outside of the core followers were driving out demons when Christ said "whoever is not against us is for us" Saul-Paul's epistles could legitimately be removed from the Bible and from church doctrine altogether. This is not true of the other books in the Bible; Saul-Paul's epistles are different and are less credible than all of the other books of the Bible.

Rules are made and rules are abundant, but not so with Christ. Unlike Saul-Paul, Christ did not convolute His own messages. Christ's messages were tough and to the point, often using relatable parables that were understandable to the willing.

Abortion

There are things the Catholic church has right, and also things the church has a bit mucked up. But abortion is one of those issues that the Catholic church has right. Matthew 19 says: "And Jesus answered and said to them, 'Because of the hardness of your heart he wrote you this precept. But from the beginning of the creation, God 'made them male and female.' 'For this reason a man shall leave his father and mother and be joined to his wife, and the two shall become one flesh'; so then they are no longer two, but one flesh. Therefore what God has joined together, let not man separate." Now, people will point out the obvious that this is referring to marriage as that is what The Christ was speaking about in that text. However, these two do in fact become one flesh in their children "Therefore what God has joined together, let not man separate", so to destroy that one flesh by ripping the baby limb from limb from its mother's womb seems to be very contrary to Creation. God is a Creator and God destroyed only when the Created fouled itself, but did so only to build anew. This abortion problem of killing the preborn is not going to end well for any of those who are directly or indirectly supporting it, even if indirectly supporting it through your vote. What will **your** defense about that be on your judgement day? What position did you take in regard to the abortion issue?

The thought of ripping you apart while you are still in your mother's womb just seems wrong on every level. While abortion is obviously wrong, making it illegal is not going to solve the problem. Sure, many children will live and not be murdered in their mother's womb and will grow to live full robust lives if abortion were to be illegal all around the world. But, unless we dive deep in to the root of the problem, the problem will persist illegally regardless.

Abortion is not the problem, though it is obviously wrong. The problem is girls becoming pregnant before being emotionally ready to have and raise a child with a committed husband. And to dig a bit deeper, the problem is people having any sexual relations at ages that they are far too young to handle the emotional weight that accompanies those sexual relationships, even if you are older it shows immaturity. This sort of intimacy should be reserved for those who are dedicated for lifelong companionship and who want to have children. If you recall, it is the act of intercourse or "knowing" one another that truly seals the marriage bond or betrothal. This means that if you have intercourse with someone but then to go on to marry someone else you are then committing adultery with the latter one you chose to marry. This is a non-negotiable truth as in Matthew 19 where "Jesus answered and said to them, 'Because of the

hardness of your heart he wrote you this precept. But from the beginning of
the creation, God 'made them male and female.' 'For this reason a man shall
leave his father and mother and be joined to his wife, and the two shall
become one flesh'; so then they are no longer two, but one flesh. Therefore
what God has joined together, let not man separate." And also "I say to you,
that whosoever shall put away his wife, except it be for fornication, and shall
marry another commits adultery, and he that shall marry her that is put away.
commits adultery." A wedding is a public ceremony that makes a
commitment in front of family, friends, and God. A "marriage" is
what that promise or commitment is about, and our modern-era
legal documents are meant to help you keep that promise.

While it is good that the church speaks out and fights against
abortion, it misses the root of the problem. Yes, Christ needs
soldiers on the abortion front-line, but if we fail to send the
troops to the youth with Truth as our battle sword, then the free-
flow of unexpected pregnancies will not only continue, but will
continue to increase regardless of whether or not abortion is
legal.

Birth Control

The Catholic church's stance on birth control is both
overreaching and completely justified. It is completely justified in
that when the birth control doctrine was established in the Trent
Catechism, birth control was a means to abort the child through
chemicals or medicines, basically an abortion pill or abortion
solution. This birth control prohibition was multi-pronged. First
is the obvious part where ending a pregnancy for your own
selfish purposes kills your child, but also to not live in a wildly
lustful way with little care for the other person you are having
relations with.

For many Catholics, this prohibition came to mean that **all**
forms of birth control are wrong and evil. This false doctrine is
derived from the misunderstood book of Tobias where an angel
told Tobias that he is to take a virgin as wife and with the fear of
the Lord have children for the love of children rather than as the

result of lust. Who can argue with that? In fact, if people only had children when they wanted them then abortion would cease to exist rather quickly. The original issue of "birth control" was not that it prevented conception; it was that medicine birth control at that time killed the little baby inside the mother. That was the heinous nature of birth control then—It was abortion! These medicines killed the child in the womb, thus breaking the Sixth Commandment. In the modern era and throughout all of human history these things occurred. Often through covetous lust people will have an illicit affair and then lie about the fact that they coveted and stole from their neighbor in this way. Then they will proceed to kill the baby they hate so much from their illicit union, and all to the disgrace of their parents. And this is aside of them most likely accusing God and cussing along the way, thus breaking nearly all of the Ten Commandments in one fell swoop.

To really grasp the birth control issue, we must first decide specifically what "birth control" is. Abstinence is considered "birth control", and so is withdrawal, which was done by Onan in the Bible when he was supposed to give his sister-in-law Tamar a child. His brother, Tamar's husband, had died and it was the custom that Onan should come together with Tamar and give her a child through his seed for his dead brother's namesake. But Onan, being the clever fellow he was, decided to do the sexual act with Tamar, but then just before completion he withdrew, spilling his seed on the ground. Some people wrongly take this as we are not to control birth in any way, but that is wrong.

Onan essentially raped his widowed sister-in-law Tamar. He was to give her a child through is his seed. However, he had sex with her, but then refused to give her his seed. His refusal to give his sister-in-law Tamar his seed was the wrong part in his actions. It is not wrong for married couples to regulate birth. Intimacy is a gift from God, but married couples must realize that regardless of any birth control methods they might use that their intimate acts can result in the conception and creation of a child.

Most married couples are fully aware of this and will love any child that arises from their intimate union whether or not they are using any sort of birth control.

When the angel spoke to Tobias, the point was not about birth control, the point was to have the child as a wanted being rather than an unwanted result of lust. Non-murderous birth control in a marriage is not wrong. Abstinence, barrier, withdrawal, and cleansing or washing are all acceptable forms of *conception-prevention* within a committed marriage, but the only one that works every time is abstinence. For the church to try to place the burden of using no means of regulating conception whatsoever within a loving married relationship is a heinous action by the Catholic church hierarchy towards the True Church of Christ and the life-long committed couples within it.

The types of "birth control" just mentioned are all **non-**murderous methods that prevent conception, but with each comes the possibility of creating a child from the activity with which it is used. And just as importantly, when a husband and wife have intimate relations, those moments should *always* be done in love and care with the natural desires God implanted in us for such activity, rather than only for lustful purposes. Then even if conception occurs, that child will be "conceived in love", and as for the "pill" or other birth control methods that alter the biochemistry so as to *prevent* conception, that is a bit on the edge of the topic and gets pretty close to going over the edge, and it's probably not our best as humans.

All other forms of controlling birth that are not mentioned in the previous paragraph are intended to end the life of the newly conceived child and are all considered abortive and are murder, thus breaking the Sixth Commandment. There is a critical distinction to be made between *conception prevention* and *birth control.*

A loving union that is committed for life should enjoy each other for the gift that they are to each other as often as they see fit. "Birth control" of a non-murderous nature is really contraceptive or *conception-prevention* and should only be used within any committed marriage **because** only committed couples should be engaging in intimate activities that would require such methods. "Birth control" should not even be discussed by the church unless they are going to explain the distinction between *conception-prevention* versus *murderous birth control methods.* It is each **married** couple's own choice as to whether or not to prevent conception, and preventing conception is **not** a sin. The unjust burden that the church has placed on the congregation demanding that **any** means of "birth control" outside of abstinence is sinful has a left an untold path of devastation between the couples within the church and in the world. This trail of tears continues and will continue as long as man's rules dominate the Catholic church. Where in the Bible does is say "Thou shalt not have intimate relations with your spouse"? And where does it say "Thou shalt not use **any** form of preventing conception within a committed marriage"? **It does not!**

The Bible is quite silent about the goings on between husband and wife other than to say that those details are between the husband and the wife and must not extend outside of that relationship or it is considered adultery and covetous.

The Catholic church's stance on "birth control" is overly broad and is dangerous and the time spent fighting such causes has shifted the focus from where it ought to be to a placed, to where it has no business. We often get caught up in fighting the result rather than the problem. In this case we have two issues coming together. If the church was be able to differentiate between *abortive-murderous-birth-control,* versus *conception-prevention* it would clear things up considerably. *Birth-control* states in its name that it is intended to alter or control birth. This means that the baby is *already* conceived, where contraception or *conception-prevention,* on the other hand, simply stops conception from occurring within the married couple until they feel ready to have children.

And if the "church" would focus on teaching the value of marriage and waiting until you are in a fully committed lifelong relationship before engaging in intimate sexual activity, then people who are not married would not be so freely engaging in such activity and thus would have no need for any *abortive-murderous-birth-control* or **abortions**, or even *conception-prevention*. Of course this is easier said than done, but resetting the focus in this way would make a considerable difference in the outcome, and it would be far more caring and loving towards the flock.

Lifestyle

When the church opines on birth-control it loses focus on the bigger picture and is essentially saying it's okay to have sex if you are not married, just don't use "birth control" when doing so. As discussed in a previous chapter, the downfall of the church began long ago during the Renaissance era with the disputes regarding the selling of indulgences in exchange for money. Vatican II and the new order mass, Novus Ordo, were not the cause of the modern era societal downfall; they were the **result** of the downfall and only served to further accelerate the situation.

Many of the points espoused by the Catholic church are dogma or principles put forth by the church authority as "incontrovertibly true", but while that is the technical description of these matters, it does not make the dogma incontrovertibly true. Just because we say something is so does not make it so. Truth will always reign supreme. Birth control became a big topic when it was made legal around the time the "pill" was concocted in the mid-nineteen-hundreds, which alters the menstruation cycle of women through chemical means. Whether you want to pin the blame of societal downfall on this nefarious method of birth control is up to you, but you are wasting your time in doing so. The free-sex movement of the "sexual revolution", as it is usually referred to, was nothing new. What was new about it was its scale in size. The various forms of birth control and the legalization thereof didn't help the situation, but certainly and provably did not cause the problem. Read history regarding the downfall of culture and you will quickly understand what is being referred to here.

The Bible and history are both filled with an endless string of sexual debauchery and have recorded the path of wreckage that such practices have left, all of which existed long before modern forms of birth control were ever invented or made illegal or legalized. In fact, modern birth control came on the scene *because* of sexual promiscuity, not the other way around.

It was the lifestyle of promiscuity that brought about birth control. Figure out the non-marital promiscuity problem and you will have eliminated the need for any sort of murderous birth control, as well as conception prevention outside of a loving marriage. The Saul-Paul doctrine has been of no assistance in this, Saul-Paul said, "To the unmarried and the widows I say that it is good for them to remain single, as I am. But if they cannot exercise self-control, they should marry. For it is better to marry than to burn with passion." Saul-Paul is saying here to marry for the sake of lust explicitly implied in "But if they cannot exercise self-control, they should marry. For it is better to marry than to <u>burn with passion</u>." However, some Bibles simply say "than to be burnt" rather than "<u>burn with passion</u>." which would likely imply that it will save them from hell, but the notion is the same. Saul-Paul is basically saying if you are lustful, then get married.

How about the two become as one just like God intended at the time of Creation? And how about we do it in the midst of love for our chosen mate? How might that bit of advice turn out rather than Saul-Paul's foolhardy idea to marry for the sake of not burning or not burning with passion, that is to say uncontrollable lusts, how about that? This particular statement of Saul-Paul's is found in 1 Corinthians 7:9 in most Bibles. And it is in this Pauline doctrinal dogma that largely has borne the idea of priests not marrying. We should have no problem with priest not marrying and remaining celibate, but we should also have no problem with priests marrying as they did in the Old Testament of the law about which Jesus The Christ said "For assuredly, I say to you, till heaven and earth pass away, one jot or one tittle will by no means pass from the law till all is fulfilled."

The Levites were the priests in the Old Testament and they had children and some of those children in turn became priests because only the Levites where allowed to be priests, thus proving clearly that priests married and had offspring. How long would the priesthood have lasted if those Levites had never married and had children? Maybe only their one generation? Yes, only a single generation! The issue of celibacy within the priesthood is a perversion of God's instructions. Celibacy could even be considered a perversion of God's commands within the general populace because the two became one flesh and were told to "Increase and multiply, and fill the Earth, and subdue it" in Genesis Chapter One. God did not demand that priests marry or have offspring, their choice to have offspring was optional, but God certainly did *not* say that priests should *not* marry. It was quite the opposite.

This foolish Pauline doctrine has brought upon the Catholic church an onslaught of corruption in the church that has specifically invited evil into the church. The sexual abuse of young children, mostly boys, by adult priests ran rampant in the church as did the abuse and luring of young men desiring to enter the seminary down a trail of disgusting behavior. This accelerated around the turn of the twenty-first century. So this Pauline doctrine infiltrated the church and permeated it so badly that many churches, to their own peril, began to hang flags and other banners of abomination that were symbols of this male with male rape in the churches, thus promoting it as somehow good and virtuous. What they did was a double abomination.

When the Earth was flooded and made anew during Noah's time, the destruction was partly the result of similar behaviors. When the elimination of evil was completed, God made a vow that the whole world would never again be destroyed all at one time by water. As a token of this promise God made a rainvow, or more familiar to most people—a "rainbow". For the spectrum of colors from that vow, or rainbow, to be used as a symbol of the sexual debauchery of wayward priests, other wayward clergy, and other wayward people can be labeled as nothing less than total and complete blasphemy, but worse yet, it is the fullness of sin. And to make matters worse, they drape it over the Cross in some churches for the entire congregation to see. If you can believe it, it does get worse. Beyond their abomination of perverting one of God's promises and draping it on the Promise of the Cross, they proceed to preach on the merits of this by proclaiming that this is somehow "love" or "loving".

Oh how far we have fallen! Woe to you! Depart from these wicked temples people of the True Church. As Jesus said: "whoever causes one of these little ones who believe in Me to sin, it would be better for him if a millstone were hung around his neck, and he were drowned in the depth of the sea." To hang such an abominable flag on the doorpost and lentil of the door to Heaven is nothing short of pure evil.

It is time for the Catholic church to abandon Saul-Paul's doctrine and finally adopt Christ's doctrine in Matthew 23, which is a bit more to the point:

"But woe to you, scribes and Pharisees, hypocrites! For you shut the kingdom of heaven in people's faces. For you neither enter yourselves nor allow those who would enter to go in. Woe to you, scribes and Pharisees, hypocrites! For you travel across sea and land to make a single proselyte, and when he becomes a proselyte, you make him twice as much a child of hell as yourselves. Woe to you, blind guides, who say, 'If anyone swears by the temple, it is nothing, but if anyone swears by the gold of the temple, he is bound by his oath.' You blind fools! For which is greater, the gold or, the temple that has made the gold sacred? And you say, 'If anyone swears by the altar, it is nothing, but if anyone swears by the gift that is on the altar, he is bound by his oath.' You blind men! For which is greater, the gift or the altar that makes the gift sacred? So whoever swears by the altar swears by it and by everything on it. And whoever swears by the temple swears by it and by him who dwells in it. And whoever swears by heaven swears by the throne of God and by him who sits upon it. Woe to you, scribes and Pharisees, hypocrites! For you tithe mint and dill and cumin, and have neglected the weightier matters of the law: justice and mercy and faithfulness. These you ought to have done, without neglecting the others. You blind guides, straining out a gnat and swallowing a camel! Woe to you, scribes and Pharisees, hypocrites! For you clean the outside of the cup and the plate, but inside they are full of greed and self-indulgence. You blind Pharisees! First clean the inside of the cup and the plate, that the outside also may be clean. Woe to you, scribes and Pharisees, hypocrites! For you are like whitewashed tombs, which outwardly appear beautiful, but within are full of dead people's bones and all uncleanness. So you also outwardly appear righteous to others, but within you are full of hypocrisy and lawlessness. Woe to you, scribes and Pharisees, hypocrites! For you build the tombs of the prophets and decorate the monuments of the righteous, saying, 'If we had lived in the days of our fathers, we would not have taken part with them in shedding the blood of the prophets.' Thus you witness against yourselves that you are sons of those who murdered the prophets. Fill up, then, the measure of your fathers. You serpents, you brood of vipers, how are you to escape being sentenced to hell? Therefore I send you prophets and wise men and scribes, some of whom you will kill and crucify, and some you will flog in your synagogues and persecute from town to town, so that on you may come all the righteous blood shed on earth, from the blood of righteous Abel to the blood of Zechariah the son of Barachiah, whom you murdered between the sanctuary and the altar. Truly, I say to you, all these things will come upon this generation."

What more can be said about this that Jesus The Christ did not say in that bit of text?

The Eucharist

Another area of doctrine that causes many people to leave the church is that of the Eucharist and the "real presence". Many outsiders look at the Catholic doctrine and have a hard time believing it, not because Jesus is believed to be present in the Eucharist, but rather because it is supposed to magically turn into Christ's human flesh upon the Consecration. Now I suppose some people would be repulsed at this due to it being considered cannibalism to eat the flesh of another human being. But the reality is that most people do not accept that it is chemically scientifically transformed into actual flesh and blood. Now if you could bring this material of the Consecration into a hospital and they would do laboratory tests to confirm that it is actual human flesh and actual human blood, *repeatedly* from week to week, then that claim would reconcile with many more people. And I suspect that even if it did test out as actual human flesh and blood yet still tasted like bread and wine that people would still take part in communion because it would then be more accurate according to the Catholic church's false doctrine that the people have been taught.

However, due to the insistence of doctrine and certain language semantics this has driven away scores of people who, like Thomas the Apostle, wanted evidence of claims. We use the term "doubting Thomas" in reference to Thomas' not believing the other Apostles, but the other Apostles also asked to see and were shown the same that Thomas was shown. Look for it and you will find it. Thus, if no such repeatable evidence is forthcoming, then we can expect the hemorrhaging of the congregation to continue as it has been doing for a very long time due to the semantics issue of the Eucharist. Some of that hemorrhaging is internal and unseen and is only made evident when the patient eventually dies and the autopsy is done. In the end we are likely to find that the death of the Catholic church was from bad or poorly explained and mostly Pauline doctrine. Sometimes the dogma overshadows the doctrine, and that dogma is usually inserted by popes or other church leaders. If you take a look at the ways in which "the real presence" is often stated, you will see two sides, and depending upon who is saying it you will see the Eucharist described differently in accord with each their own interpretation.

One way is to say "the real presence in the Eucharist." Another is to call it "The actual Body and Blood of Christ." This understanding can be a bit nuanced, but if a human body can contain a soul then why not a piece of bread, after all, bread is one of the things that almost every one eats as a growing child, therefore, we are at least partly made of bread and we contain a soul. Thus, if we believe in God then it should not be a stretch for us to believe that the Spirit of Truth, the actual Word of God, could inhabit the communal bread upon Consecration. This is simple enough and I can imagine that most people who at the very least have a desire to believe in God can accept that part at face value without it compromising the more scientific side of their minds.

But we will take this a bit further and still not violate science. Jesus took some bread and he broke it and gave it to his disciples and told them to take it and eat it and that it was his body, but only after he had blessed it. So I ask you, do you know what an automobile is? And for most adults the answer is going to be "yes, obviously." An odd question is it not? Does that automobile have a body? Is it alive? No it is not alive, yet, it has a body as indicated in the term "body shop" where you take a car to be repaired when it has been in an accident. We have no problem whatsoever admitting a car has a body, so we should have no problem accepting that the communion "host" is also a body. In fact it is the "host" for Christ, much like a place that is "hosting" a party.

The communion bread is the place where The Living Word is believed to descend into at the time of Consecration. So no one who was brought up under the universal Liturgy should have any problem whatsoever understanding or believing that. So what part of the car is the body? It is the outside, but with the communion wafer-bread it's so thin that it doesn't seem to have an inside. Yet, if you lay one down on the table and place a drop of water on it where exactly does the water go? It is no longer on top, and did not drop below, and did not evaporate, so where did it go? It did, in fact, soak inside of the Communion bread wafer that now has become the host to the water and can also host the Living Word of God. Now if you were to place a drop of the vino onto the host you would have the body, and also the blood of the vine in the bread.

But what we don't have is something that will repeatedly test as actual human flesh and blood. We don't need to pretend that the host magically turns in to actual human flesh and actual human blood. The bread and vino are only symbolic and they are the symbols that Jesus The Christ chose to use. Neither the church nor the skeptic should have any problem with any of this.

We cannot deny that wine is the blood of the vine, nor that the communion wafer bread can contain something such as water. Therefore those two substances in that form are, in fact, in the vernacular of most cultures a body and blood, but of what?

The only point of somewhat blind trust here is that upon consecration The Living Word inhabits that body and blood. And if that actually does occur, then it would technically be the body and blood of The Living Word of God inside of that Host, yet not chemically actual human flesh and blood. But since it is not visually evident that it is being inhabited by the "real presence", some people will still doubt.

A question in this is if a church is practicing abominations and "consecrating" the bread, then do we imagine that The Word of God is now going to be present in that host where such abominations are practiced? It does not seem likely. And further, we are not supposed to eat food offered to idols, so when abominations are set up in a church building and draped over a cross or crucifix, then what or who are we consecrating the bread and wine to?

"The Real Presence" has nothing to do with the bread and wine testing out as actual human flesh and blood. It has to do with Christ, The Living Word of God, actually being present and inhabiting that Bread and Wine which we then consume and thus take into us The Living Word and The Christ. This does not diminish the Eucharist, nor negate any miracles that may or may not have occurred surrounding the Eucharist. It also has no effect on the reverence that everyone ought to have surrounding it. What it does do is to make things more of a true reality for most people when the absolute and logical Truth is conveyed rather than hocus-pocus beliefs. If you believe that humans have any sort of spirit or soul within them and if you believe that there is a higher power, typically referred to as "God", then you should have no problem with accepting that The Living Word could inhabit the communion bread wafers with "real presence" upon Consecration.

The Primary Anchors of the Catholic Church

With the political and cultural climate increasingly becoming more heathen than Heaven, the universal churches have been fighting ever harder to combat the crashing society and crashing universal church within all sects—none are exempt. The Catholic church is not alone in this. The fight against abortion and against same-gendered intimate relations and the fight against birth control and the fight to insist that the Consecrated bread is actual testable human flesh in some churches are all the wrong battles to be fighting. It's not that there should not be pushback surrounding some of these things, or that they should or should not be questioned, but rather the problem is that we spend all of our mental and physical and spiritual resources on these things, which is a sign that we missed the real problem to begin with. And we missed the problem because we have been taught lies. Tares have been sown into the wheat of Truth leading us astray for a *very* long time.

If we do not soon depart from the doctrine of Saul-Paul and the doctrine derived from the perversion of the Biblical text borne out of the Reformation era, then all will be lost. Some Catholics believe that we must stick to the current church doctrine rather than basing the doctrine on the Bible. People feel this way because that is how the Reformation actually began, it was defiance of certain church doctrine and dogma, so people are reluctant to go down that path again because doing so would only cause more splintering of the church.

The truth of the matter is that there is little that needs to change with regard to the older traditional Liturgy of the Mass. It is the underlying teaching that has been missing or incorrect, and it appears that a vast amount of true understanding is absent in the modern priesthood. Let us come together and discuss these things like adults instead of acting like a bunch of misbehaven rival teenagers having gang fights while taking part in all sorts of other debauchery, all while believing the lies that society and local culture are telling us.

Chapter 21

So Many Religions

It's easy to understand that there would be many religions in a world with no central God figure. But to see many religions from a greater universal sect who all claim allegiance to the same Creator God is a bit puzzling. If each religion is supposedly reading the same basic Bible text and the Christian religions are supposed to be serving the same God, then why oh why is there any more than one singular Christian religion?

Recognize But Resist

Because we demanded that Moses allow divorce due to our unsettling adulterous arrogant nature, those who believe "my way is the way" choose to not get along. Our arrogance causes us to divorce reality from Truth, and along with that goes our marriages, but that is only some of the people in the congregation. There are many true people in the congregation who are stable and have been keeping themselves pure while watching many shepherds fall into sin. As we witness this fall from grace, we see not only rampant sin on the part of some of these shepherds, but we also experience the erred teaching they have been promoting. Being as respectful as is reasonably possible, we can recognize their given place in the church hierarchy, but we can also resist any incorrect or unjust impositions they place upon us, of which there are far too many. These incorrect and unjust impositions have deep and long lasting ramifications for us and our families and for our futures. We must follow Christ's Truth.

That Other Church over There

The "universal" church group has fragmented itself through our arrogant stiff-necked ever-accusing and ever-unforgiving attitude, thus causing the fractures spoken of so far throughout this book. With many preachers and pastors it is *they over there* who are wrong, wrong, wrong! Oddly it is seldom ourselves who are wrong, wrong, wrong! As the saying goes "there are bigger fish to fry" than the current infighting that has been raging for centuries. It's time to move on.

But beware and use caution when attempting to reassemble the universal church into a collective whole, for if you do not use much caution, you will get caught in an inescapable snare of a one world religion. If you have not yet recognized that this is already underway right in front of your very eyes, then please do awaken from your deadly slumber. Our disjointed unity of backbiting in the universal church's various sects will feel right when we are told to reunite in some sort of international "revival" of religion. We have for so long been trained incorrectly in the doctrines and dogma in most sects, thus preparing us for our own demise. This has happened to a point where we will believe almost anything about religion that the priests and preachers tell us if it sounds and feels good to us. We get the warm-fuzzies, and we like it because it soothes our egos when any sect welcomes us and embraces our ideas and allows us to continue in our error. **Beware of a "one world church"!**

A day is coming when you will be very, very grateful that you opened up your heart to allow the Spirit of Truth to enter into you and fill you overflowing. For if you fail to do this it is certain that you will be deceived into a new world religion that will promote itself as true and good, but actually is an imposter church of wolves dressed in sheep's clothing. The deception regarding this will be so great that you will think you are serving God while doing so; however, you will be serving Satan.

Only those who know and have Truth within them will be able to discern the difference between Christ's one True Church and the false one-world church that will very possibly come through the existing fragmented church. Both will be universal in their doctrine, but only one will have a doctrine of Truth, the other will have a doctrine of lies disguised as truth.

Those Lutherans, Those Catholics

The finger pointing of the various sects must end before the problem gets so bad that none from those congregations will be saved. The story of the rift between the Catholics and the Lutherans and all of the subdivisions thereof has been spoken of throughout this book and also in the book *Understanding The Bible*. It is a common rift that has been occurring since Adam and Eve and Satan created the rift between them and God. If you happened to have friends that are either Catholic or Lutheran and you happen to be of the other religion, you will know full well what is being conveyed here. Many of us have heard or have been involved in these religious conversations with little or no progress in either direction. This is also true between any two of the vast number of universal sects.

Oddly, we disagree on petty semantics; in fact it is those semantics that caused the rifts in the first place. There are some instances where there are core differences that are not reconcilable through semantics, but those are rare. Yet it all depends upon the interpretation of the doctrine and dogma by each person as to the importance of the disputed detail.

Catholic Church

The idea of the Catholic church being referred to as "Catholic" or "Universal" is that no matter where you go you will meet people with shared beliefs. Much the way restaurant chains work where you can be relatively certain to get the same experience regardless of which location you go to within a given chain. That is how embedded into our world the church is. It is to a point that even business models itself after the church. The True Church is common or universal, and all who want Truth and repent of their sins and go forth and sin no more are welcome in The Christ's True Universal Church.

You can be very certain that any church who welcomes you in and supports your sin is a church of Satan that is built upon lies that are disguised as good. And further, you can be very certain that they will not allow the Light of Truth to enter—not even a little bit. They will say the words with their mouths, but will not harbor those words within their hearts.

Catholic Religion

What is "religion" anyway? "Religion" doesn't really exist in the way we imagine it does. Our view of religion, as we see it in the modern era, is false. Many words in our vocabulary quickly become labels and lose their actual meaning. The term "religion" means to *rebind* or *reconnect*. *Re-ligion* is like the binding ligament in your arm that connects your body to your arm.

The so-called "Catholic" religion is intended to be the tie that binds and keeps us universal via the Catholic doctrine in the Catechism. But how has that been working out in recent times? Not so well around the turn of the twentieth century, give or take several decades. The Catholic church and the Catholic religion are two parts of the same thing. The "Church" as mentioned in an earlier chapter is the *ecclesia* or the *congregation; it is the people*, that is to say *us*. The "religion" on the other hand is the doctrine or beliefs that those people follow and hold dear. Few Catholics or other universal sects truly fully know their own religious doctrine.

Catholic Faith

The "Catholic church" is *who* believes. The "Catholic religion" is *what* they believe. And the "Catholic Faith" is *how* or *why* they believe. The word faith basically means to be true to something, like, for instance, a faithful husband or faithful wife. The Catholic faith means to be faithful to the Catholic way. It is not about the *what* or the *who*, but rather the choice you make and the dedication thereof. This trio is true of any sect, or basically anything you follow *and* in the way you live your life. It is the "religion" part that is most troublesome to us.

What Religion was Moses?

Few people will get the question right with their first answer when asked, "What religion was Moses?" Is this a trick question? No, not really, rather it is a question of true Biblical awareness and acute understanding of what religion actually is. If you are unable to wrap your head around this question and its answer then you will likely miss a few points being made in the Bible's text that not many people seem to grasp. You have probably already arrived at the obvious common answer in your head, but you are most likely incorrect. So what religion was Moses? I'm not going to tell. I dare you to try to figure it out on your own *without* asking anyone or looking it up in any book other than the actual printed paper Bible that is probably collecting dust across the room in most homes.

If you should choose to accept this mission to know Moses' religion, be aware that every preacher I have ever heard talk about this has it absolutely and utterly wrong. Going to the world with such questions is going to return to you only the world's answers. But opening up your heart and mind and allowing the Spirit of Truth to overflow in you will produce more answers than you can comprehend in your lifetime.

Who is Not With Me is Against Me

We must be ever on guard because we have to remember that we live in Satan's dominion. Because we lack Truth in us, we often cannot tell whose message has Truth and whose does not. There is a bit of a perceived conflict in the Bible in some things Jesus said.

In Matthew Chapter 12 Jesus says: "Whoever is not with me is against me, and whoever does not gather with me scatters. And so I tell you, every kind of sin and slander can be forgiven, but blasphemy against the Spirit will not be forgiven. Anyone who speaks a word against the Son of Man will be forgiven, but anyone who speaks against the Holy Spirit will not be forgiven, either in this age or in the age to come."

But then in Mark Chapter 9 Jesus says: "Do not stop him, For no one who does a miracle in my name can in the next moment say anything bad about me, for whoever is not against us is for us. Truly I tell you, anyone who gives you a cup of water in my name because you belong to the Messiah will certainly not lose their reward."

In one place Jesus says "whoever is not with me is against me" and in another place He says "for whoever is not against us is for us." Both of these are very contextual statements having to do with the surrounding circumstances. In the modern era, if someone has not chosen to side with you then they will ultimately be against you. The context of a given situation will make one or the other of these statements true for most people who are involved in great controversy or conflict. In the first case in Matthew 12, Christ is speaking of those doing evil, but in the second case in Mark 9 he is referring to someone who is doing good but is not specifically one of the Apostles. That person is doing good and is not against them so it benefits their cause. Where in the other case if the person is not working for the cause and is also doing evil, then that person doing evil is not for Him and is working against Him.

The "If they are not for you they are against you" situation is also true in the modern era, because in the modern era most subjects are so divisive as to force everyone to one side or the other. Thus they will either be with you or will sell you out for their own protection. If they turn on you, then they will likely not get attacked like you will be attacked when you stand for Truth. But according to the Bible, hellfire is their abode because if you have embraced Truth, but they reject that Truth, then they have sealed their doom.

Protect yourself against this error by consuming The Spirit of Truth with all of your heart, and all of your mind, and all or your soul—You will not regret doing so. Whoever is not for you will most likely work against you to save their own reputation, their ego, and their skin. But if someone is doing good things that benefit you and your cause, even if you do not know them, as long as they are not against you, then they are working with you and to the benefit of your cause.

Chapter 22

So Many Choices

Life is a long series of choices that only we get to make. Society can make something illegal, like abortion for instance, and if we hate children so much and hate ourselves we will seek that abortion regardless of the law or religion. What we really need to abort from our lives are the works of Satan.

Absent of Light

Satan was called "Lucifer". We think of Lucifer in a bad way but the term means the bearer of light. It is truly a sad choice that Lucifer made in defying God, thus becoming a "fallen angel". Yes Lucifer, that is to say Satan, is indeed an angel, but now is an angel of darkness who rules over this lower world. But lest you misunderstand it will be repeated again. The lower world is the one that is submissive to the higher realm, which is to say *our* lower realm or our world. Satan is who controls the realm that we live in as flesh and blood. This world truly lacks the Light of Truth. You can find it when looking for Truth, but most people hide their light for fear of ridicule from the world and for fear of attacks from Satan.

The Christ said "You are the light of the world. A city that is set on a hill cannot be hidden. Nor do they light a lamp and put it under a basket, but on a lampstand, and it gives light to all who are in the house. Let your light so shine before men, that they may see your good works and glorify your Father in heaven." This comes and goes, but the trend in modern times is to hide our light for fear of personal character attack. So it is important that we remember that The Christ also said this: "But whoever denies me before men, I also will deny before my Father who is in heaven." That is a *very* clear notification for us, and it is wise for us to remember it.

The Fire Within the Angel of Light

Lucifer was arrogant and overzealous. He was to bow in reverence to man who was made in the image of God, but instead sought to make himself above man, and for this he was cast out of Heaven into the lower Earthly realm. The angel of light has a fire within, but the fire was for himself and for his arrogance, rather than for God. In his effort to be above Adam and Eve, he ended up making himself even lower than even his angelic counterparts.

But understanding how God works and how all things work for a common purpose, even if we cannot see that or understand it, God most likely knew that the power of choice endowed to Lucifer would potentially and very likely be abused. This situation is the awareness of freewill.

"Original Sin"

Lucifer did seal the doom of his stature through his defiance. The Angel of Light had to be cast down to the earthly realm because evil and inferior substance cannot be contained in the Heavenly realm. Satan's only goal was to place himself above Adam. Now, since Adam was Created slightly above the angels with him being made explicitly in the image of God, there is no way for Satan to be above Adam's originally created position or state. The hierarchical position of the Created cannot rise above what it was created as, but it can fall below. Lucifer fell below, which gave him an opportunity to drag Adam down a few notches along with him. All Satan had to do was to find a means by which to have Adam and Eve submit to him, thus making his position above Adam's position, or rather Adam's position subordinate to Satan. If only he could find a way to do this...

This is where the Garden of Eden and the Tree of the Knowledge of Good and Evil comes into the picture. Satan the Serpent knew that Adam and Eve did not know that there was a difference between Good and Evil. He knew that they would be as vulnerable as a three-year-old in this regard by the very nature of them not knowing between good and evil. So, when Eve came near the Tree of the Knowledge of Good and Evil, all Satan had to do was to merely suggest that it is good and that it was not a big deal and that she would benefit from it. Satan knew that Adam and Eve would likely take his bait and step right into his trap of submission due to their innocence, and so they did.

Our Choices are Our Freedom Versus Freedom is Choice

It seems unfair for God to have allowed Satan to take advantage of these young innocent vulnerable souls, but free will is a tricky subject that has many ups and many downs. Adam and Eve's submission to Satan, or their Original Sin, did not make us wanton and week, it made us culpable for our errors. Prior to the Original Sin of submission to Satan, rather than submission to God, Adam and Eve could have done absolutely anything and not had to experience death of soul, but since they contracted with Satan through their actions, they were now under Satan's power. And Satan's jealousy and hatred is so intense that he sought their death or imprisonment as well as that of all of man to come.

Our Original Sin defect is unavoidably buried in our DNA in the same way that our fingers, toes, and eyes are. This Original Sin might have turned out slightly different had Adam and Eve done so of their own accord. In that case they might still have had to face death, but they possibly would not have had to be under the submission of Satan. Our Original Sin did indeed make us more like God by way of knowing between Good and Evil, but it also made us impure. This is why we need to be washed by accepting The Blood of the Lamb of God and repent of all of our sins that we now know are wrong as we commit them. We are aware and therefore are guilty because we now know. Guilt is like being gilded or covered in something; in this case it is being covered in the particular sin offence and darkness.

The Anathema

An Anathema is a ban or curse pronounced by ecclesiastical authority followed by excommunication. Some of these terms we hear bandied about in the Catholic church are somewhat disturbing. For instance, the idea that the Pope would pronounce a curse on someone is disturbing. Should a pope not rather be calling down blessings of enlightenment on such troubled individuals? The Catholic church is well on its way to becoming its own anathema, for it has indeed cursed itself and submitted itself to the wiles of Satan. But that is the Catholic and universal church sects. It is not the True Church of The Christ. There is great confusion in all of this because the True Church of The Christ is in fact Universal, and people in the True Church of The Christ do attend services at the various universal sects' churches. But those sects are not the same thing as Christ's True Church.

What is Sin?

Sin is sometimes tough to discern. We often consider it a sin to break the Mosaic Laws, those guidelines set forth in the Old Testament that are in addition to the Ten Commandments. The

Pharisees insisted that the people were sinning if they did things such as eating swine flesh, but that was not specifically a sin, rather it simply made you unclean for a short time. The term "*sin*" means *without*, or *void*, or *empty*, or *not*. Sin is anything we do that separates us from God. Certainly some things are more severely sinful, but not all things that seem bad for us in God's eyes are specifically sins. This is why Jesus was always getting upset with the Scribes and Pharisees. Their legalistic lies were convicting innocent people of sin that were merely unclean where they only needed to take certain simple actions to be clean again, many of which are simply good hygienic practices. True sin is to separate ourselves from God and be void of The Spirit of God in any way.

Purgatory

What is purgatory? "Purgatory" is a term that was invented sometime around the twelfth-century, implying the purging of sin from our souls. Purgatory is believed to be a place or state of *being* that we go to be cleansed of our stubborn ways. There are many things that we might very well have wrong about hell and purgatory and the lake of fire. We must remember that in the Bible in Revelation it states that "Death and Hell will be thrown into the lake of fire where there will be wailing and the gnashing of teeth." We always interpret that as hell and hell-fire, but it is not. Hell is not as intense as that and it is very possible that what we think of as hell is the same as the idea of "purgatory". The Bible appears to indicate that the righteous offspring of Adam and Eve who would accept the Promise of God would be resurrected when Jesus Died and went to Hell then Arose from the dead, and at that time the righteous arose also, and then later they were taken to Heaven.

The righteous who die *after* The Christ's Death, Resurrection, and Ascension will sleep until sometime around the second coming. It might be that purgatory is that time period between the first and second coming of The Christ if purgatory is actually a real thing. The term "purgatory" is not mentioned or implied in the Bible, it is an invented theory of mankind implying a purging of sin. And it is very possible that purgatory is simply what we think of as "hell", which is described as unpleasant.

Christ or the Pope?

At some point, every Catholic or any other universal sect member must decide if we will follow the Pope and other leaders, or will we follow Jesus The Christ who is The Living Word of God? There is no way to financially buy into this deal because it is free of charge for all of mankind—and it can be done in an instant. But following Christ can have some costs to your worldly experience. Doing so could cost you your family and friends. It could cost you your job and your status. It could potentially even cost you your life as has happened to so many before you.

The Christ told us that his way would have costs, but for those who are willing to pay the price, the benefits you will gain are Joy and life everlasting. We should all choose The Christ's ways rather than the Pope's ways. This does not mean that we toss away all things "Catholic". It means that we actually adhere to the True Liturgy of the Mass and are sent forth to do our work for The Christ. We are to do so while ignoring and rejecting those things that we know are not in accord with The Christ's words regardless of what we believe we think Saul-Paul said. Choose Christ instead of Saul-Paul and choose The Truth of The Christ's ways always!

Chapter 23

Does the Church Matter?

As we near the end of this quest to understand the church, most notably the Catholic church, we must ask, does it matter? Does the Catholic or any other church matter? I suppose it all depends upon one's perspective on things. We can ask in the sense where we question "Has it affected you?", then in that case the answer is without hesitation, "Yes!" There is nowhere on this earth and nothing within western culture that has not been affected in some way, no matter how remote of a connection, by the churches and the doctrine thereof. So yes, in that case it is obvious that the church mattered to us.

But does the church matter to your soul? On the surface that is one of those perspective questions. Some people believe it is all fantasy and that the church is wasting its time, but while that is a possibility, it is highly unlikely. In this case it is only in the person's mind that the church doesn't matter. The church matters no matter what we choose to believe, because there is a Creator God whether we choose to believe it or not. But we have the

Bible, so then why does the church and its doctrine matter if we have the Bible?

The Catholic church is what has brought the Bible through many centuries, and while people might not want to accepted this, there is nothing in western society that the church has not had some amount of influence on, no matter how small. Without the persistence of the church you would likely not be here to read this book or a Bible. However, The Christ's True Church are the True vessels of Truth. Christ's True Church is not some organization that makes manmade rules that defy Christ's Words and instructions, nor is Christ's True Church a bunch of authoritarians who administer the organization. Every church building could collapse; and every single member of the clergy could suddenly die, including the Pope; and every holy book of writ could be burned—but The True Church of The Christ will still be alive and well and probably the better for it. The only exception is the True Liturgy which is to say The Bible which we need in order to pass the Good news on to our children of each successive generation. The Bible tells us about The Christ and our Salvation.

Obedience to the Church?

The Catholic machine has an authority problem where the hierarchal clergy, and unfortunately the laity, mistakenly believe that the Vatican along with its management system of Priests, Bishops, Cardinals, and the Pope as a whole *are* the Catholic church—But they are not! Much like a government of the people by the people and for the people, the True Church of The Christ is also of the people by the people and for the people in order to bring us close to God so that we can be at one with God.

The Catholic church demands the congregation's obedience to the church and to the Popes, and if you don't fall in line then you just might get cast out. Your opinion has no place in the world's Catholic church. Certainly no church should be run like some democracy. But the church is made up of the people within it. The Catholic way implies that the Pope is not to be defied and only his opinion counts. Recall what happened to Galileo. Recall the Reformation. Recall what happened to priests and bishops early in the twenty-first century. Obey and fall in line, or they will cast you out!

Don't Ask Too Many Questions

There is an implication that we ought not to ask too many questions. We can ask questions, but those questions best not challenge the Pauline doctrine that has been wrongly inserted into the church. We even get this at home as children. "You ask too many questions" we are told, and then that gets reinforced by teachers and preachers etc. as we age. When we finally come of age and start to ponder the deeper questions of life, like questions that might challenge church doctrine, we then get the same message that we "should not ask too many questions".

We are told "some things are supposed to be accepted on faith alone". The dangers of this wrong thinking are discussed in *Understanding Prayer*. It is time for people to realize that all of the evidence is right before our eyes, thus there is little need for blind faith, and little need to adhere to the foolish and defiant part of the doctrine of the Catechism that was mentioned earlier pertaining to believing in faith and not questioning things in the doctrine. This is completely contrary to Christ's Words when he said, "Ask and it will be given to you; seek and you will find; knock and the door will be opened to you. For everyone who asks, receives; the one who seeks finds; and to the one who knocks, the door will be opened" We are commanded by The Christ Himself to be inquisitive and anyone telling us to not question things is not to be trusted. Denying true things is far different than questioning things in effort to better understand them.

We Fail to Ask

Because of the lifelong discouragement that we get when we ask tough questions, we often fail to ask anything at all as we age. When we ask questions that people have the answers for or things they are right about they are all too happy to answer our tough questions. But what happens when those answers are wrong or inaccurate or even unavailable? When people cannot answer questions with proof of evidence a couple of situations typically arise: First they might withdraw because they simply do not know and don't want to look foolish, so in this case their withdrawal is a place for them to hide, rather than simply admitting that they do not know some things. Another thing that happens is that we ask questions because we see flaws in the statements that someone is making; in this case our questions are a challenge to their knowledge. If we persist it will frustrate and anger them because they do not have answers to questions that reveal any holes in their logic. This often results in their belligerence and mockery towards us.

True logic must balance all aspects of a subject. If things are not making sense and don't reconcile, then someone is usually cheating in their logic by ignoring things that don't fit with their desired outcome. This all usually provokes them to lash out, or to try to silence or embarrass you so that you stop with your incessant probing questions—But don't stop until Truth is revealed!

Ask and You Shall Receive

You must train yourself to ignore people's belligerence in your quest for Truth, for if you acquiesce to their belligerent behavior you will never find Truth that you seek. The Christ said "Ask and it will be given to you." The Christ wants you to form a question in your mind—and then ask it.

We often see young people trying to be rebellious as they imitate people who challenge erred authority. But that is a wrong idea and a wrong approach. We need not challenge authority for the sake of challenging authority; we need to challenge authority's *errors* when we see obvious conflicts in their statements or in the doctrine that they are trying to impose upon us.

We are told that we should ask and we will receive. Christ wants us to be curious and to be ever seeking Truth, all while rejecting things that are contradictory to Truth. We are also told by The Christ to not be double-minded. When we disassociate two conflicting thoughts that are attached to the same issue, we are double-minded and are in conflict in our thinking which is irrational and unhealthy for us, as is discussed in *Understanding Prayer*. All things must balance and be in harmony or something is either wrong in our thinking or we are missing some data. The only way to test our thinking is to ask questions surrounding the topic of conflict, and the only way to find the missing data is to ask more questions as needed.

In The Christ's statement, "Ask and it will be given to you; seek and you will find; knock and the door will be opened to you. For everyone who asks, receives; the one who seeks finds; and to the one who knocks, the door will be opened", we see *asking*, *seeking*, and *knocking*. These are all very similar functions as they all are a *quest*, but they do differ.

Seek and You Shall Find

"Asking" is a simple verbal function and it is first in line of action. The function of "seeking" is an active action on your part to go out and find the answer to something you want to ask about. "Knocking" is the most active function that has you standing at the door of the answers.

You can ask God "Where are you?" and maybe you will get a "Here I am" answer back, but seeking is specifically going forth to look for God by following that voice. Knocking occurs when you find the door on which to knock after you have found where what you are looking for is located.

First we ask "where is the door?" Then we realize that we must find the door, and then when we get to that door we must knock on it. Christ is that door and it is our Liturgy to be the Mass (or our work to go forth and share that information). Once we have found our quest, then we are to teach that Liturgy to others whether in bulk to a group or only to our family and friends. On the other side of the door is the Paradise of being **atoned** with The Glorious Word of God—our Creator.

Chapter 24

An Eternal Church

Christ's True Church will never end because it is Eternal. However, the Catholic church as we think of it will end. The term Catechism means to teach and the content of a Catechism is what we are told to teach. But should we?

Catholic Dogma

Catholic dogma is the things that the Catholic church hierarchy deems are true, which includes the Catholic catechism. This does not mean that it is true, but rather just that the Catholic church claims that the information is true. Much of it is true, but some dogma could be wrong, as discussed throughout this book.

The True Catechism is the Bible and the True dogma is the Gospel, and The Christ's True Church is comprised of all of those who do God's will and accept and believe the True Catechism and the True dogma and seek Truth and accept Jesus The Christ's Sacrifice for your Salvation. It does not matter if you are baptized as a Catholic or a Lutheran or were baptized into some other universal sect. If you are truly following the Good Shepherd you are a part of the True Universal Church of The Christ.

Is There Salvation Without the "Catholic" church?

Can you receive the Salvation offered by The Christ without the Catholic church? Yes you can, but you cannot without being a part of Christ's True Catholic/Universal Church. We are that Church, it does not matter what religion or faith you were baptized in or brought up in so long as you follow Christ's ways and adhere to **His** Catechism. Christ's True Catholic Church consists of many good Catholic church shepherd-priests and other clergy who currently work under the Vatican's sometimes nefarious leadership, as well as good clergy from other universal sects, and it also includes us—the laity. The not-so-universal Catholic church is to be credited for carrying the Bible and the Liturgy through the centuries, but it is those who are a part of the True Eternal Catholic Church that work within the world's Catholic church who are the ones largely responsible for the carrying forward of the True Catechism of the Gospels.

The Promise of Eternal Truth

We were Promised by God that the Word would come to save all of Adam and Eve's offspring of which everyone who has ever lived, and who is alive now, and who will live in the future are beneficiaries of that Promise. We have an eternal Promise that we can possess the Eternal Truth of God. And with it comes certain wonderful benefits.

Life Eternal

When we repent and are made clean with the Pure Blood of the Lamb of God we then receive the Promise of Eternal Truth. This Truth is our pathway or Gate or door to Eternal Life. Without The Living Word of Truth we cannot enter into the

Heavenly realm. The Heavenly realm is a scientifically plausible level of existence that has its own type of "physical" above or beyond our realm, so it appears intangible and invisible to us, and thus, we cannot detect Heaven "scientifically".

Was Christ's Gruesome Death a Big Deal?

An earlier chapter mentioned the purpose of the Cross with its shape and its purpose in being made of the wood from a Tree, just like the Tree of the Knowledge of Good and Evil was wood. Also mentioned, as written in other ancient documents complimentary to the Bible, was how Adam was seriously injured by Satan maybe even killed and brought back to life by God's Word, and then Adam offered his blood up to God with full purity of heart. God being so touched at this offering told Adam that he would take on him all of the sorts of sufferings that happened to Adam to be done as a sign for us to know the Promise was being fulfilled when the time was to come.

So was Christ's gruesome death a big deal? In a comparative manner, not particularly. Many people have suffered very gruesome deaths at the hands of maniacs. But Christ's death was particularly gruesome and coupled with all of God's very specific indicators, it made that gruesome death very important for all of us. So, it wasn't the *manner* of death in itself that was a big deal, it was the fact that the death was in accordance with what God told Adam; this made it all a very big deal for everyone on Earth. If we should choose the path of being a part of The Christ's **True** Universal/Catholic Church it is a very big deal to us because through it all we will be with God for eternity. We will live in the Light of Peace and Joy forever.

But Christ's death is almost a bigger deal to those who reject the Eternal Promise, because if they reject it they will spend eternity "in the Lake of fire where there will be weeping and gnashing of teeth." The part that makes this worse is that when we choose that path we must understand that our perception of the passage of time is relative to our experience and to our circumstances. Eternity will move along at a good perceived pace when you are in Heaven, but our perception of time seems to slow down when we are faced with traumatic circumstances. This means that not only will each moment seem excruciatingly long, but it also means that those excruciatingly long moments of torment will continue for eternity. It seems here then that your best option in that case will be to pray in order to forget your defiance as a point of comfort during your torment, if that is possible.

It is your choice if you happen to be undecided as you sit on the fence about whether or not to believe the things that are discussed in this book. It is your own choice using the free will that God bestowed upon you at your conception. But know this: while we might want to point fingers at God as we say things like "How could a loving God do that to His creatures?", you must understand that what *is*, is what *is*, and if God Created everything, then once your soul is created in your mother's womb you are officially a soul, a spirit being. And when a soul is created there is no way for the soul to no longer exist. This means that you are permanently here–*forever*! This is likely not some contrived torment Created by God for our torture, but rather God invented a method for us to Create souls and to do so in our own image. Once those souls have been created, there is no way to eliminate them. ***You will be conscious forever*** with no end in sight. If this is true, then our choice as to how we each want to spend that eternity is a very big deal indeed!

To add to this, if you have read *The Science of God Vol 1* discussing the first four days of Creation regarding the astrophysics aspects of Creation, you will be aware of the division of the superior and submissive states of Created heaven and earth, that is to say the above and below states. This knowledge gives you a glimpse into the reality that there is a real tangible Heaven, which our own tangible realm is intermingled within. Maybe God did make the lake of fire for tormenting sinners, but it's possible that the lake of fire is an ongoing result of Creation that will become the final abode for the unrepentant.

It is true that God gets angry with us, but that's more along the lines of a parent who is angry at us for something stupid we did, where we might get spanked as a child, but God is not going to deliberately torture us just for the sake of eternally torturing us.

I suspect that the lake of fire is the only option. There appears to be an indication that at some point our lower realm will "pass away". If this occurs, then what other options are there? What if science is right and the sun and other stars are limited in how long they are going to last and this lower realm has a limited lifespan? What if Heaven in its purity is the only pleasing place left? What if the byproduct of the passing Earthly realm is a massive burning lake of fire and brimstone? What if it is not a punishment but it's simply not physically or spiritually possible for any sort of uncleanness to enter into Heaven? What if it is not God's choice but rather is a result of God's Creation? What if unclean unrepentant people can't enter Heaven because only pure things can enter Heaven so they must stay outside, and the lake of fire is the only remaining possible location, and a soul cannot be un-Created? What then?

Then is God some megalomaniacal bully, or is God loving and caring for trying to get the importance into our stubborn stiff-necked heads in order to get all of us into Heaven? I say this because this seems to be the sort of thing the Bible is indicating. Jesus The Christ told us "And if your eye causes you to stumble, pluck it out. It is better for you to enter the kingdom of God with one eye than to have two eyes and be cast into hell where the worms that eat them do not die, and the fire is not quenched."

If you say to someone "I am warning you", do they take it as a threat, or do they take it as a notification of danger? Their answer to that question may very well be an indication of where they will end up if you are not able to get through to them with your warning. Is God threatening us, or is God trying to help us?

We each make this decision on our own, and it is each our own decision to be *at one* with the True Church of Christ–The True Church of Christ being the Pure Bride *at one* in The Spirit of Truth with the Groom Jesus The Christ. Will you become a part of the One True Universal Catholic Church that follows the Good Shepherd and serves God? If you do then you truly are *Understanding The Church*.

A Creed of Aspects of God

I know there is One God The Creator who conceived all things and brought them into existence by raising them up to a higher state. God Created a way when the Spirit of God separated the light from the darkness and separated the waters above from the waters below. When God separated the water above from the waters below, Earth was, and then the waters below were gathered embracing all matter. God's commitment to the firmament holds all things in place. We are offered by God the Creator with an open hand, to be guided to the waters of the life-spring where all mankind can share in the same. We have been given ears with which to hear, eyes with which to see, mouths with which to speak, desire with which to quest, and a mind with which to learn and remember. For we represent the Living God and it is up to you to decide to ask questions and find the free and Eternal Promise of Truth through The Living Word of God who is the Groom, of the Bride who is the True Catholic Church of The Christ.

Christ said "For this was I born, and for this came I into the world; that I should give testimony to the Truth. Every one that is of the Truth, hears <u>my</u> voice." When we are of Truth and Hear The Christ's voice and follow The Christ's commands then...

<u>We</u> are the Bride,
<u>We</u> are the True Universal Church of Christ!

Understanding The Bible

The Bible How-To Manual
AND
The Things We Don't See

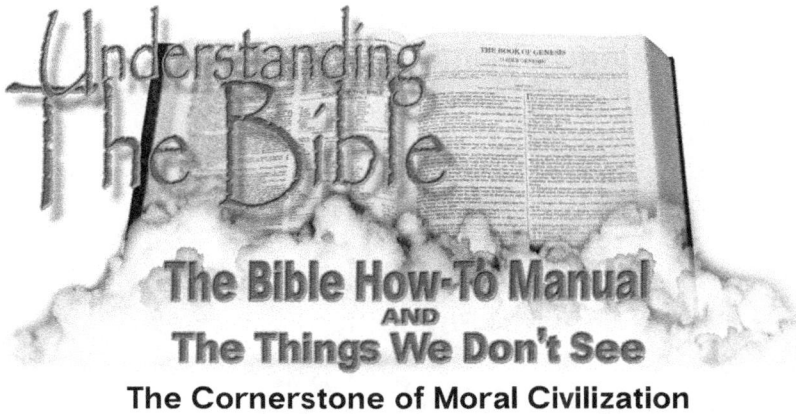

The Cornerstone of Moral Civilization

Was Jesus really the "Savior"? Did Noah really save humanity from extinction? Did Adam and Eve really get evicted from the Garden of Eden? And what does the word "Bible" mean anyway? When studying or even just reading the Bible, many questions arise to a point where the Bible can be confusing. But when you have certain information before you begin reading, it can instantly propel you to a deeper level of understanding by nothing more than knowing a few key points.

It takes people years to realize some of this information, yet it's not some big secret that only scholars and theologians know. No, this information is for everyone and it's easy to grasp these pieces of information about the Bible and some of the events described within it. Be prepared to have your current views challenged because many things are not as we have been taught.

To truly Understand the Bible, we must open our minds and toss aside all of our biases. Knowing and grasping the often-unrealized basic information presented in *Understanding The Bible - The Bible How-To Manual and The Things We Don't See* brings the Bible to life in a way that shows you, personally, its undeniable relevance to the world, to our culture, and to your very own life!

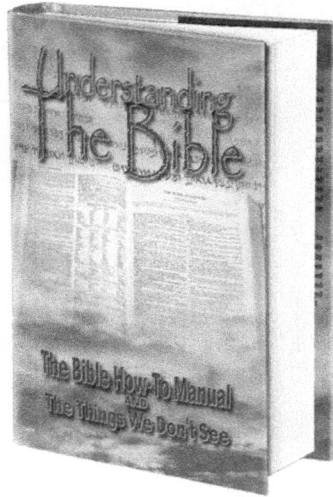

Search: Understanding The Bible Book
SayItBooks.com

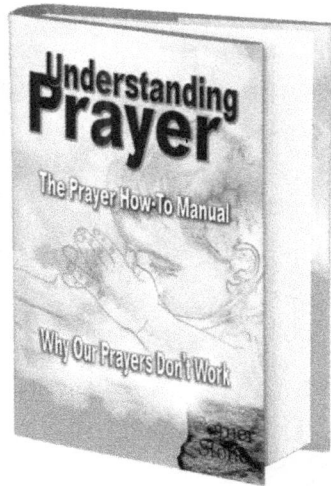

The Science of God
Volume 1
The First Four Days

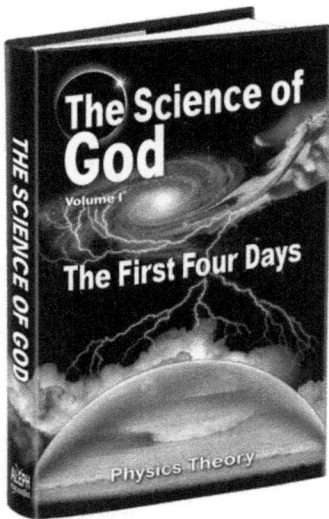

Volume 1 - The First Four Days

THE SCIENCE OF GOD

The Science of God
Volume 1
The First Four Days

Physics Theory

Is there a God? Did we evolve? Did everything start from a big bang? These questions have been plaguing our minds for many years. Only science-minded people and clergy seem to have the answers. But do they really have any true answers?

Is what we are told by science true? Is what we are told by the Church true? Or are there other better explanations for everything? Did we hitch a ride from Mars, or is that all fantasy science? Was everything created in six twenty-four hour days, or did it all take billions of years to happen? Few people are willing to even fully consider these questions, and even fewer have any coherent answers. *The Science of God Volume 1 – The First Four Days* challenges your current beliefs while asking tough questions of science and of the Church.

For years, Christian after Christian has attempted to argue for God and the Bible's Creation only to fail miserably. Why is this, why is it that Christians cannot seem to win this debate? Often Christians think they are winning the debate only to find themselves at a loss to answer the real questions, and then they get mocked for their poor answers.

Whether you are a scientist or an average Christian and want to discuss the Creation debate, *The Science of God Volume 1 – The First Four Days* is a mandatory read for you. *The Science of God* takes you through the thought process to enable you to speak intelligibly about Creation, the cosmos, evolution, and astrophysics.

Search: The Science Of God Book Volume 1
SayItBooks.com

Rocking the Cradle of Life
A Decent Account of Descent

Have you ever wondered if humans actually did evolve from apes? Or maybe, if we were specifically created, then how might have that occurred? There sure are a lot of opinions on the evolution versus creation topic. And too often these views use confusing technical jargon that few people care to learn or have ever even heard.

The answers to the questions you might have are, in many cases, the same answers that many other people seek. When you have solid answers that are difficult for someone to thwart, it's good to share those answers so that others can also feel confident with their own understanding of the arrival of mankind and the level of importance that it has in their own lives.

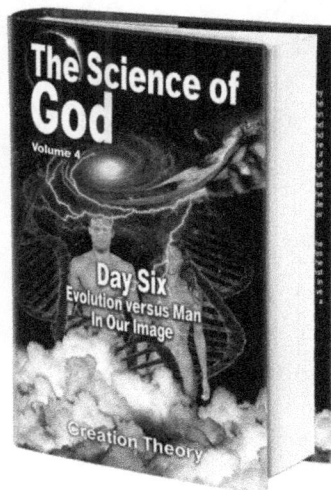

The Science Of God Volume 4 - Evolution versus Man – In Our Image takes a deep but simple dive into the human evolution versus human creation debate using simple language that everyone can understand and enjoy!

If you have thoughts that you have been reluctant to share, then suspend your thoughts for a bit and open your mind to consider the perspectives and evidence presented in *The Science Of God Volume 4 - Evolution versus Man – In Our Image*. You will acquire a much clearer view of the subject as you read the various points made in this engaging book about the arrival of mankind.

Search: The Science Of God Book Volume 4
SayItBooks.com

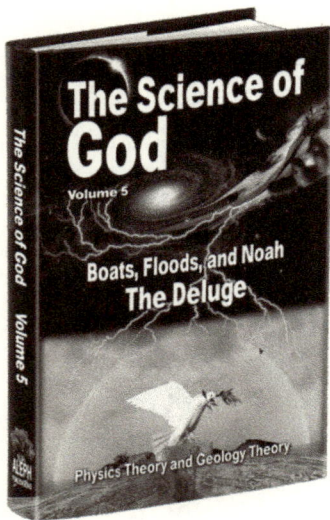

When You Dream... DREAM THIN™
The Weightloss Repair Manual

Learn How to Lose Weight While Sleeping

How many people do you know who exercise and still can't seem to lose weight? Has that ever happened to you? As a matter of fact, because we don't know the vital secrets that are shared in *Dream Thin*, many of us actually end up *gaining* weight when we exercise.

Do you hit your weight loss goals? And does your weight stay off when you do actually lose some weight? Even many doctors miss the *real* answers to weight loss. If you doubt this, then simply look at the waistlines of many medical doctors and nurses.

Weight loss is easily mastered when you understand a few basic principles. We often go on fad diets or follow the orders of our doctors, only to put the weight back on even faster than we lost it. Many of us suffer from unnecessary disease, and some of us will die too young.

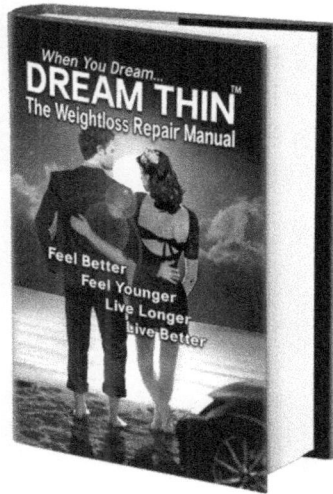

Dream Thin does more than simply share answers to weight loss mysteries. *Dream Thin* explains the important details of *why* and *how* weight loss connects to mind and body. The information in *Dream Thin* allows you to make weight loss permanent without having to try so hard. Don't make more of the same empty promises to yourself each New Year's Day. Instead, quickly and easily change things today and make all of your tomorrows better with *Dream Thin* while still enjoying all of the foods you eat today—and yes, even fast foods!

Only you can choose if you want spend your hard-earned money on medical bills and funerals, or if you would rather spend your time and money looking great while being out and about and enjoying life with friends and family as intended!

Search: Dream Thin Book
SayItBooks.com

Notes

Notes

Notes

Notes

Notes

* 9 7 8 1 9 5 6 8 1 4 3 6 1 *